The ESSENTIALS® of
REGISTERED TRADEMARK

GER

D0720534

Linda Thomas, Ph.D.

Associate Professor of German
Randolph-Macon Woman's College
Lynchburg, Virginia

Research and Education Association
61 Ethel Road West
Piscataway, New Jersey 08854

THE ESSENTIALS®
OF GERMAN

Printed in the United States of America

Library of Congress Catalog Card Number 94-65500

International Standard Book Number 0-87891-927-9

ESSENTIALS is a registered trademark of
Research & Education Association, Piscataway, New Jersey 08854

WHAT "THE ESSENTIALS" WILL DO FOR YOU

This book is a review and study guide. It is comprehensive and it is concise.

It helps in preparing for exams, in doing homework, and remains a handy reference source at all times.

It condenses the vast amount of detail characteristic of the subject matter and summarizes the **essentials** of the field.

It will thus save hours of study and preparation time.

The book provides quick access to the important principles, vocabulary, grammar, and structures in the language.

Materials needed for exams can be reviewed in summary form – eliminating the need to read and re-read many pages of textbook and class notes. The summaries will even tend to bring detail to mind that had been previously read or noted.

This "ESSENTIALS" book has been prepared by an expert in the field, and has been carefully reviewed to assure accuracy and maximum usefulness.

Dr. Max Fogiel
Program Director

Contents

vii

CHAPTER 1

Alphabet and Sounds

1.1 The Alphabet

There is only one letter in the German alphabet that does not exist in the English alphabet: ß. This letter was originally an *s* and a *z* and is named after those two letters, ***ess-tset.***

a ah	*g* geh	*m* emm	*s* ess	*w* weh
b beh	*h* hah	*n* enn	*ß* ess-tset	*x* iks
c tseh	*i* ih	*o* oh	*t* teh	*y* üppsilon
d deh	*j* jot	*p* peh	*u* uh	*z* tsett
e eh	*k* kah	*q* kuh	*v* fau	
f eff	*l* ell	*r* err		

1.2 Vowels

Vowels are long when followed by an *h* or by only one consonant. They are short when followed by two or more consonants.

a	long (as in father)	*Vater*
	short (as in part)	*kalt*

e	long (as in obey)	*geht*
	short (as in met)	*Bett*

i	long (as in machine)	*ihm*
	short (as in hit)	*ist*

o	long (as in go)	*Hof*
	short (as in bought)	*Gott*

u	long (as in pool)	*Schule*
	short (as in bull)	*Mutter*

1.3 Modified Vowels

An umlaut (¨) modifies the sound of a vowel. In some cases there is no corresponding English sound.

$ä$	long (as in air)	*Käse*
	short (as in yet)	*Männer*

$ö$	long (similar to worm)	*schön*
	short	*öffnen*

$ü$	long	*Tür*
	short	*müssen*

1.4 Diphthongs

Diphthongs are always long.

ai, ei (as in mine)	*Hain, dein*
au (as in house)	*Maus*
eu, äu (as in boy)	*Leute, Bäume*
ie (as in see)	*die*

1.5 Consonants

b	initial (as in English)	*baden*
	final (like **p**)	*Dieb*

2

c	before **a, o, u,** (like **k**)	*Cousin*
	before **i, e, y,** and an umlaut (like **ts**)	*Cent*

ch	after **a, o, u,** (no English equivalent)	*Buch*
	after **i, e,** an umlaut and consonants (like English **h** in hew)	*möchte*

chs	(like **ks**)	*sechs*
ck	(like **k**)	*Ecke*

d	initial (as in English)	*du*
	final (like **t**)	*Bad*

f	(as in English)	*fahren*

g	initial (like English **go**)	*gut*
	final (like **k**)	*Tag*

h	initial (like English **he**)	*haben*
	after long vowel (silent)	*sehen*

j	(like **y**)	*ja*
k	(as in English)	*kann*
kn	(both are pronounced)	*Knie*
l	(like English **lit**)	*lieben*
m, n, p	(as in English)	*Mann, nein, Platz*
ng	(like English **sing**)	*Finger*

pf	(both are pronounced)	*Pfanne*
ph	(like **f**)	*Philosophie*
qu	(like **kv**)	*Quelle*
r	(uvular)	*rot*
s	initial and between vowels (like English **rose**)	*lesen*
	final, before consonants and when doubled (like English **son**)	*essen*
ß	(like English **less**)	*heiß*
sch	(like English **shoe**)	*Schuh*
sp	(like **shp**)	*springen*
st	(like **sht**)	*stehen*
t	(as in English)	*tun*
th	(like **t**)	*Theater*
ti	(before a vowel, **tsi**)	*Nation*
tz	(like **ts**)	*Katze*
v	(like **f**)	*Vater*
w	(like **v**)	*Wasser*
x	(as in English)	*Hexe*
z	(like **ts**)	*zehn*

4

CHAPTER 2

Cases

German has four cases. Without an understanding of the function of each case, it is impossible to proceed with German grammar.

2.1 The Nominative Case

The nominative case is the subject case. The subject of the sentence performs the action expressed by the verb. It tells us who or what performs the action.

Der Hund hat den Mann gebissen. **The dog** bit the man.

The verbs *heißen, sein,* and *werden* can never have an object. They are always followed by the nominative case. One should think of these verbs as an equal sign. The nouns on both sides of the equation are nominative.

Nom.   Nom.
Er heißt   *Herr Schmidt.* His name is/He is called Mr. Schmidt.
Er ist   *unser Lehrer.* He is our teacher.
Sie wird *die beste Schülerin der Klasse.* She is becoming the best pupil in the class.

2.2 The Accusative Case

The accusative case is the direct object case. The direct object receives the action performed by the subject and expressed by the verb. It answers the question "who?" or "what?" after the verb.

*Der Hund hat **den Mann** gebissen.* The dog bit **the man.**

In English, grammatical function often is shown by word order. The meaning of the English sentence can be changed drastically by changing the word order.

The man bit the dog.

In German, the article indicates the case and a change in word order cannot change the basic meaning.

***Den Mann** hat **der Hund** gebissen.* The dog bit the man.

Den shows that ***Mann*** is the direct object (accusative), and ***der*** shows us that ***Hund*** is the subject (nominative). Putting the direct object first does change the emphasis.

The accusative case also functions as the object of the prepositions ***durch, für, gegen, ohne,*** and ***um.*** This will be discussed further in chapter 10.

2.3 The Dative Case

The dative case is the indirect object case. It answers the question "to whom?" after the verb. Unlike English, which signals the indirect object by a preposition or by word order, German changes the form of the article, pronoun, or noun.

*Der Mann hat **dem Hund** einen Knochen gegeben.* The man gave a bone **to the dog.**/The man gave **the dog** a bone.
*Der Hund hat **dem Mann** einen Ball gegeben.* The dog gave a ball **to the man.**

The dative case also functions as the object of the prepositions ***aus, außer, bei, mit, nach, seit, von,*** and ***zu*** (discussed in chapter 10). In addition, the dative case is used with certain verbs. Some of the most common are *antworten, danken, gefallen, gehören, helfen,* and *zuhören.*

> *Er antwortet **mir**.* He is answering me.
> *Wir danken **dir**.* We thank you.
> *Diese Musik gefällt **mir**.* I like this music. [Literally: This music is pleasing to me.]
> *Die Bücher gehören **ihm**.* The books belong to him.
> *Kannst du **ihr** helfen?* Can you help her?
> *Du hörst **mir** nie zu.* You never listen to me.

2.4   The Genitive Case

The genitive case is used to show possession or the relationship between two objects. This is often achieved in English with an apostrophe. Sometimes the equivalent English expression uses "of the," "of a," "of my," and so on.

> *Der Mann hat den Knochen **des Hundes**.* The man has the dog's bone.

Proper names form the genitive by adding an *-s* with no apostrophe, unless they end in *-s.*

> *Johanns Mutter kommt heute.* Johann's mother is coming today.
> *Das ist Hans' Adresse.* That is Hans' address.

The genitive case also functions as the object of the prepositions *(an)statt, trotz, während,* and *wegen.* Examples will be given in chapter 10.

CHAPTER 3

Articles

3.1 The Definite Article

In English, the definite article "the" is used to designate specific nouns. The use of the definite article in German is almost the same as in English. However, in contrast to the English definite article, which has only one form, the German form changes according to gender, number, and case. The forms must be memorized.

	Masculine	Feminine	Neuter	Plural
Nominative	*der*	*die*	*das*	*die*
Accusative	*den*	*die*	***das***	*die*
Dative	*dem*	***der***	*dem*	*den*
Genitive	*des*	*der*	*des*	***der***

The articles in bold type appear in the following example.

***Der*[1]** *Mann gibt* ***der*[2]** *Mutter* ***der*[3]** *Kinder* ***das*[4]** *Foto.* The man gives the photo to the mother of the children.

[1] masc. nom.   [2] fem. dat.

[3] gen. pl.   [4] neut. acc.

3.1.1 *der*-Words

The following words are known as "*der*-words" because they follow the same pattern as the definite article.

dieser (this, these), *jeder* (each, every), *mancher* (many a, several, some), *solcher* (such), and *welcher* (which). *Jeder* is singular. The plural is *alle,* which also takes the endings of the definite article in the plural. *Mancher* and *solcher* are both usually plural.

> *Dieser Mann gibt jeder Mutter solcher Kinder dieses Foto.* This man gives this photo to every mother of such children.
> *Jede Frau bekommt ein Foto.* Each woman receives a photo.
> „*Alle Menschen werden Brüder."* "All men become brothers."
> *Manche Frauen bekommen solche Fotos.* Some women receive such photos.

3.2 The Indefinite Article

In English, the indefinite article "a, an" is less specific than the definite article. It is used, for example, to discuss **a** book rather than a specific book (**the** book). In contrast to English, which has only the forms "a" or "an," the German form changes according to gender, case, and number. Obviously, there is no plural form, (one cannot have "a books"). However, the plural of *kein,* which follows the same singular pattern as the indefinite article and negates nouns, is usually included in paradigms of the indefinite article.

	Masculine	Feminine	Neuter	(Plural)
Nominative	*ein*	*eine*	*ein*	*(keine)*
Accusative	*einen*	*eine*	*ein*	*(keine)*
Dative	*einem*	*einer*	*einem*	*(keinen)*
Genitive	*eines*	*einer*	*eines*	*(keiner)*

9

Ein[1] Mann gibt einer[2] Mutter eines[3] Kindes ein[4] Foto. A man gives a mother of a child a photo. *Keine[5] Kinder bekommen ein Foto.* No children receive a photo.

| [1] (masc. nom.) | [3] (neut. gen.) | [5] (pl. nom.) |
| [2] (fem. dat.) | [4] (neut. acc.) | |

The use of the indefinite article in German is almost the same as in English. A notable exception is the omission of the indefinite article in German before names of nationalities and professions.

Er ist Amerikaner. He is an American.
Sie ist Professorin. She is a professor.

3.2.1 *ein*-Words

Possessive adjectives are known as "*ein*-words" because they follow the same pattern as the indefinite article and the negative *kein*. The possessive adjectives are *mein* (my), *dein* (your), *sein* (his, its), *ihr* (her, its), *unser* (our), *euer* (your), *ihr* (their), and *Ihr* (your).

Ihr Mann gibt seiner Mutter unser Foto meines Kindes. Her husband is giving our photo of my child to his mother.

The singular of *solcher* is usually *so ein.* In this construction, the *ein* is declined according to case and gender.

Ihr Mann gibt seiner Mutter ein Foto so eines Kindes. Her husband is giving his mother a photo of such a child.

10

CHAPTER 4

Nouns

4.1 Gender

All nouns in German are capitalized and are either masculine *(der)*, feminine *(die)*, or neuter *(das)*. In the plural, the article is *die* regardless of gender. Most nouns referring to males are masculine and most referring to females are feminine. Days, months, and seasons are masculine.

der Mann the man/husband
der Vater the father
die Frau the woman/wife
die Mutter the mother

The ending *-in* can often be added to the masculine noun to form a feminine noun.

der Professor the professor
die Professorin the female professor
der Student the student
die Studentin the female student

Unfortunately, the gender of a noun is often illogical; therefore, nouns should be memorized with their articles. Mark Twain poked fun at German because the nouns for "young girl" *(das Mädchen)* and "young lady" *(das Fräulein)* are neuter.

However, there are some guidelines that one can follow, as those two nouns illustrate.

All nouns ending in *-lein* or *-chen* are neuter. These two suffixes make diminutives of nouns.

All nouns ending in *-heit, -keit, -ie, -ik, -ion, -schaft, -tät,* and *-ung* are feminine.

die Kindheit childhood
die Freundschaft friendship
die Melodie melody

Most nouns ending in *-e* are feminine.

die Katze cat
die Note grade
die Woche week

Most countries, such as *Deutschland,* are neuter. Articles are seldom used with countries or cities. Two notable exceptions are *die Schweiz* (Switzerland) and *die Türkei* (Turkey).

4.2   Plurals

The formation of plurals in German is varied and not always predictable. It might be best simply to learn the plural when learning the noun and the article (gender), as the following possibilities for forming plurals will make clear.

Some nouns make no change in the plural.

Singular	Plural
das Theater the theater	*die Theater* the theaters
der Onkel the uncle	*die Onkel* the uncles

Most nouns ending in **-el** add an umlaut and have no ending in the plural.

der Mantel the coat *keine Mäntel* no coats

Some nouns add an **-e** in the plural.

das Bier the beer *die Biere* the beers

Some nouns add an umlaut and an **-e** in the plural.

der Sohn the son *die Söhne* the sons

Some nouns add an **-er** in the plural.

das Bild the picture *keine Bilder* no pictures

Some nouns add an umlaut and an **-er** in the plural.

der Mann the man/husband
  die Männer the men/husbands

Approximately eighty percent of the one-syllable masculine and neuter nouns add an **-e** or an **-er** in the plural and some also have an umlaut.

Some nouns add an **-en** in the plural.

die Frau the woman/wife *keine Frauen* no women/wives

Some nouns add an **-n** in the plural.

die Woche the week *die Wochen* the weeks

This rule applies to approximately ninety percent of all feminine nouns. The exceptions are usually names of animals.

die Kuh the cow   *die Kühe* the cows
die Maus the mouse   *die Mäuse* the mice

Some nouns, usually of foreign origin, add an *-s* in the plural.

das Auto the car   *die Autos* the cars

Feminine nouns formed by adding *-in* to the masculine, add *-nen* to form the plural.

die Professorinnen the female professors
die Studentinnen the female students

One final note: in the dative plural, all masculine and neuter nouns add an *-n* unless the plural form already ends in *-n* or *-s*.

Der Mann gibt den Kindern die Fotos. The man gives the photos to the children.

4.3   Compound Nouns

A compound noun in German can consist of two or more nouns.

*die **Hand*** (hand) + *der **Schuh*** (shoe) = *der **Handschuh*** (the glove)
*das **Jahr*** (year) + *die **Zeit*** (time) = *die **Jahreszeit*** (the season)
*die **Sonne*** (sun) + *der **Strahl*** (beam) = *der **Sonnenstrahl*** (the sunbeam)
*das **Leben*** (life) + *die **Versicherung*** (insurance) + *die **Gesellschaft*** (company) = die *Lebensversicherungsgesellschaft* (the life insurance company)

A compound noun can also consist of a verb and a noun.

schreiben (to write) + *die **Maschine*** = *die **Schreibmaschine*** (the typewriter)

14

A compound noun can consist of an adjective and a noun.

neu (new) + *das Jahr* (year) = *das Neujahr* (the new year)

Notice that the gender of the compound noun is determined by the final noun. The connectives *-(e)s-*, *-(e)n-* are common, but there are no rules for their use.

4.4   Masculine *N*-Nouns

Some masculine nouns have an ending of *-n* or *-en* in all cases except the nominative. In dictionaries this ending is given before the plural ending. Here are some of the most common.

der Herr, -n, -en the gentleman
der Nachbar, -n, -n the neighbor
der Junge, -n, -n the boy
der Tourist, -en, -en the tourist
der Mensch, -en, -en the man, human being
der Student, -en, -en the student

Der Student sagte „guten Morgen" zu seinem Nachbarn. The
    student said "good morning" to his neighbor.
Der Herr gab dem Studenten das Buch. The man gave the book
    to the student.

4.5   Masculine and Neuter Nouns in the Genitive

Masculine and neuter nouns add an *-es* ending in the genitive singular if they are one syllable and an *-s* if they consist of more than one syllable.

Er ist der Sohn dieses Mannes. He is the son of this man.
Das ist das Auto meines Onkels. That is my uncle's car.
Wie ist der Zustand des Fensters? What is the condition of the
    window?

As stated in the preceding section, masculine N-nouns end in *-n* or *-en* in all cases except the nominative. In the genitive, a few also add an *-s*. The most common of these is *der Name*.

Was ist die Herkunft des Namens? What is the origin of the name?

4.6   Negation of Nouns

Nouns with no article and nouns preceded by the indefinite article are negated by using *kein*. *Kein* is declined like the indefinite article.

Wir haben Geld. Wir haben kein Geld. We have money. We have no money.
Sie bringt einen Kuchen. Sie bringt keinen Kuchen. She is bringing a cake. She is not bringing any cake.

But
Sie bringt den Kuchen. Sie bringt den Kuchen nicht. She is bringing **the** cake. She is not bringing the cake.

CHAPTER 5

Pronouns

5.1   Personal Pronouns

The personal pronoun for "you" in German often causes problems for the English speaker. The familiar form for "you" has both a singular *(du)* and a plural *(ihr)* form. The familiar form is used with family members, children up to the age of fourteen, and animals. Students address each other with the familiar form. The formal form of "you" *(Sie)* has the same form for both singular and plural and is capitalized in all cases. The capitalization is important, because it is often the only distinguishing characteristic between the pronoun *sie* (they) and *Sie* (you) in written German. In conversation, only the context makes the meaning clear.

Kommen sie mit Ihnen? Are **they** coming with **you?**
Kommen Sie mit ihnen? Are **you** coming with **them?**
Kommen sie mit ihnen? Are **they** coming with **them?**

The pronoun for "she" is also *sie* and can be distinguished by the verb ending from *sie* meaning "they."

Wann kommt sie? When is she coming?
Wann kommen sie? When are they coming?

17

Personal pronouns stand for nouns and must agree in gender and number with the nouns to which they refer. English speakers tend to use the German pronoun *es* in all cases when it corresponds to "it." *Es* is correct only if the noun referred to is neuter. Otherwise, *sie* (she, it) and *er* (he, it) must be used if the noun referred to is feminine *(sie)* or masculine *(er)*.

> *Wie findest du **die Farbe**? **Sie** ist schön.* How do you like the color? It is beautiful.
>
> ***Der** Dom ist schön. Ja, **er** ist herrlich.* The cathedral is beautiful. Yes, it is magnificent.
>
> *Wie ist **das Buch**? **Es** ist sehr interessant.* How is the book? It is very interesting.

PERSONAL PRONOUNS
SINGULAR

Nominative		Accusative		Dative	
ich	I	*mich*	me	*mir*	to me
du	you, fam.	*dich*	you	*dir*	to you
Sie	you, form.	*Sie*	you	*Ihnen*	to you
er	he, it	*ihn*	him	*ihm*	to him
sie	she, it	*sie*	her, it	*ihr*	to her, to it
es	it	*es*	it	*ihm*	to him, to it

PLURAL

Nominative		Accusative		Dative	
wir	we	*uns*	us	*uns*	to us
ihr	you, fam.	*euch*	you	*euch*	to you
Sie	you, form.	*Sie*	you	*Ihnen*	to you
sie	they	*sie*	them	*ihnen*	to them

Notice that there are personal pronouns for all cases except the genitive.

5.2   Reflexive Pronouns

A reflexive pronoun refers back to and is identical with the subject. English uses the suffixes "-self" or "-selves" to form reflexive pronouns. German reflexive pronouns are identical with the accusative and dative personal pronouns except in the third-person singular and plural. In the third-person singular and plural and in the dative and accusative, the reflexive pronoun is *sich.*

> *Er wäscht sich.* He is washing himself.
> *Sie waschen sich.* They are washing themselves.

In the case of the other reflexive pronouns, one must often decide whether to use the direct or indirect object pronoun. If there is another direct object (accusative) in the sentence, the reflexive pronoun must be in the dative case.

> *Ich wasche mich.* I am washing myself.
> *Ich wasche mir die Hände.* I am washing my hands.

In contrast to English, it is grammatically incorrect in German to use possessive adjectives when referring to parts of the body. Nevertheless, in the spoken language possessive adjectives are being used in this context more and more frequently.

5.3   Relative Pronouns

Relative pronouns relate a subordinate clause (relative clause) to a main clause by referring back to a noun in the main clause.

> She is the woman **who** was here yesterday.

The noun to which the relative pronoun refers is known as its antecedent. In German, the relative pronoun must agree with its antecedent in gender and number. The case is determined by its use in the relative clause.

> *Sie ist die Frau, die gestern hier war.* She is the woman **who** was

19

here yesterday.

Er ist der Mann, dem ich das Buch gab. He is the man **to whom** I gave the book.

In the first example, the relative pronoun *die* is feminine because it refers to *die Frau,* and it is nominative because it serves as the subject of the relative clause. In the second example, the relative pronoun *dem* is masculine because it refers to *der Mann,* and it is dative because it is the dative object in the relative clause.

When the meaning of the relative pronoun is "whose," it is genitive no matter what its grammatical function in the relative clause, but it still must agree in gender with its antecedent.

Sie ist die Frau, in deren Haus ich wohnte. She is the woman in **whose** house I lived.

Note that in German, a relative clause is always set off by a comma.

The form of the relative pronoun is almost the same as that of the definite article. In the paradigm below, the deviations from the definite article are shown in bold type.

RELATIVE PRONOUNS

	Masculine	Feminine	Neuter	Plural
Nominative	*der*	*die*	*das*	*die*
Accusative	*den*	*die*	*das*	*die*
Dative	*dem*	*der*	*dem*	*denen*
Genitive	*dessen*	*deren*	*dessen*	*deren*

5.4 Indefinite Relative Pronouns

When the antecedent of a relative pronoun is an unspecified person, the appropriate form of the interrogative pronouns *wer* (nom.), *wen* (acc.), *wem* (dat.), or *wessen* (gen.) is used.

Ich weiß nicht, wer kommt. I don't know who is coming.
Ich weiß nicht, wen sie sah. I don't know who she saw.

*Ich weiß nicht, **wem** er das Buch gab.* I don't know to whom he gave the book.

*Ich weiß nicht, **wessen** Buch das ist.* I don't know whose book that is.

The indefinite relative pronoun *was* is used:

(a) when the antecedent of a relative pronoun is an unspecified thing.

> *Hast du gesehen, **was** er getan hat?* Did you see what he did?

(b) when the antecedent of a relative pronoun is a superlative adjective used as a neuter noun.

> *Es war das Beste, **was** ich machen konnte.* It was the best that I could do.

(c) when the antecedent of a relative pronoun is an indefinite pronoun such as ***alles, vieles, manches, etwas, wenig, or nichts.***

> *Nicht **alles, was** er sagte, war interessant.* Not everything that he said was interesting.
> *Aber **etwas, was** er uns zeigte, war doch interessant.* But something that he showed us was interesting after all.

(d) when the antecedent of a relative pronoun is an entire main clause.

> *Sie meint, er kann nicht kommen, **was** ich nicht glaube.* She thinks he can't come, which I do not believe.

5.5   *da(r)*- and *wo(r)*-Compounds

A preposition + a pronoun referring to a thing is always replaced by a ***da(r)***-construction. The *r* is inserted before a vowel.

Das Buch war interessant. Sie sprechen darüber. The book was interesting. They are talking about it.

(über + es = darüber)

This happens only when the pronoun refers to a thing. If it refers to a person, it remains unchanged.

Der Professor war interessant. Sie sprechen über ihn. The professor was interesting. They are talking about him.

The interrogative *was?* + a preposition is replaced by the *wo(r)*-construction.

Wovon/Worüber sprechen sie? What are they talking about?

(was? + von = wovon; was? + über = worüber)

The interrogative, *was?* always refers to a thing. If the reference is to a person, the correct form of *wer?* is used.

Von wem sprechen sie? Who are they talking about?

CHAPTER 6

Verbs

6.1 About Verbs in General

The basic form of a verb is the infinitive. Most infinitives in German end in *-en,* but some end in *-n.* The stem of a verb consists of the infinitive minus the *-en* or *-n* ending. German has three types of verbs: regular, irregular, and mixed. Regular verbs simply add endings to the stem to form the present and simple past tenses. Irregular verbs have a vowel change in one or both of these tenses. Mixed verbs not only have a vowel change in the past tense but also add a past-tense ending.

6.2 The Use of the Present Tense *(das Präsens)*

The present tense is used more extensively in German than in English. It is often used, for example, where the future would be used in English. If the sentence contains an adverb indicating that the future is intended, the present tense is preferred.

Ich fliege morgen nach Berlin. I will fly to Berlin tomorrow.

The present tense is also used to express an event that began in the past but is still continuing.

Er wohnt seit einem Jahr in Berlin. He has been living in Berlin for a year.

It is important to remember that whereas English has three present-tense forms, German has only one.

I **do** that.
I **am doing** that. } *Ich mache das.*
I **do do** that.

6.2.1 The Formation of the Present Tense (Regular Verbs)

The paradigms below illustrate the present-tense endings of the regular verbs *machen* (to do) and *arbeiten* (to work).

Singular	**Plural**
Ich mache das.	*Wir machen das.*
Du machst das.	*Ihr macht das.*
Sie machen das.	
Er/Sie/Es macht das.	*Sie machen das.*

Verbs like *arbeiten* that have stems ending in *-d* or *-t,* insert an *-e* before the ending to aid pronunciation of *du, er, sie,* and *es* forms.

Ich arbeite.	*Wir arbeiten.*
Du arbeitest.	*Ihr arbeitet.*
Sie arbeiten.	
Er/Sie/Es arbeitet.	*Sie arbeiten.*

6.2.2 The Formation of the Present Tense (Irregular Verbs)

Irregular verbs change the stem vowel in the second- and third-person singular.

sehen (to see)

Ich sehe ihn.	*Wir sehen ihn.*
Du siehst ihn.	*Ihr seht ihn.*
Sie sehen ihn.	
Er/Sie/Es sieht ihn.	*Sie sehen ihn.*

Sometimes the vowel change is in the form of an umlaut.

schlafen (to sleep)

Ich schlafe.	*Wir schlafen.*
Du schläfst.	*Ihr schlaft.*
Sie schlafen.	
Er/Sie/Es schläft.	*Sie schlafen.*

The present tense of the verb *sein* (to be) is completely irregular.

*Ich **bin** Student.*	*Wir **sind** Studenten.*
*Du **bist** Student.*	*Ihr **seid** Studenten.*
*Sie **sind** Student/Studenten.*	
*Er/Sie/Es **ist** Student(in).*	*Sie **sind** Studenten.*

The verb *haben* is irregular in the second- and third-person singular.

*Du **hast** kein Geld.* You have no money.
*Er **hat** kein Geld.* He has no money.

6.2.3   The Formation of the Present Tense (Modals)

Modal auxiliary verbs modify the meaning of other verbs and express ideas such as desire, obligation, ability, and permission. Modals must be used with an infinitive, either expressed or understood. They stand alone only if the meaning of the other verb is clearly understood. In English, one can say "I can" or "I must" if something in the conversation tells us what one can or must do. The same is true in German.

*Er **kann** heute kommen.* He can come today. (is able to)
*Er **darf** heute kommen.* He may come today. (is allowed to)
***Soll** er heute kommen?* Is he supposed to come today?
*Ja, er **soll**.* Yes, he is supposed to.

Modals in German are irregular in the singular of the present tense and must be learned. Since the plural follows the regular pattern of present-tense conjugations, it will only be given in the first example below.

Dürfen
to be allowed to, to have permission to

*Ich **darf** lange schlafen.*	*Wir **dürfen** lange schlafen.*
*Du **darfst** lange schlafen.*	*Ihr **dürft** lange schlafen.*
	*Sie **dürfen** lange schlafen.*
*Er/Sie/Es **darf** lange schlafen.*	*Sie **dürfen** lange schlafen.*

Können
to be able to

*Ich **kann** kommen.*
*Du **kannst** kommen.*
*Er/Sie/Es **kann** kommen.*

Müssen
to have to

*Ich **muß** kommen.*
*Du **mußt** kommen.*
*Er/Sie/Es **muß** kommen.*

Sollen
to be supposed to

*Ich **soll** kommen.*
*Du **sollst** kommen.*
*Er/Sie/Es **soll** kommen.*

Wollen
to want to

*Ich **will** kommen.*
*Du **willst** kommen.*
*Er/Sie/Es **will** kommen.*

The subjunctive form of ***mögen*** (to like to) is used far more frequently than its present-tense form. It corresponds to English "would like." Like modals, it has a dependent infinitive.

26

*Ich **möchte** kommen.*
*Du **möchtest** kommen.*
*Er/Sie/Es **möchte** kommen.*

6.3 The Imperative

In English, the imperative has only two forms.

Go home early today.
Let's go home early today.

In German, the imperative is a bit more complicated. The first of the English examples above can be expressed in German in three ways.

Gehen Sie heute früh nach Hause! (formal singular and plural)
Geh heute früh nach Hause! (informal singular)
Geht heute früh nach Hause! (informal plural)

6.3.1 The Formation of the Imperative

As the examples above illustrate, the formal imperative is simply the **verb + *Sie***. The verb comes first. In German, the imperative is punctuated with an exclamation point.

The informal singular imperative has no pronoun. It consists of the *du* form of the verb without the ending.

*(du) geh(st) = **Geh!*** Go!

If the *du* form is irregular and has added an umlaut, the umlaut is dropped.

*(du) läufst schnell = **Lauf** schnell!* Run fast!

The informal plural *ihr* imperative is simply the verb without the pronoun. It is used when speaking to more than two people with whom you are on familiar terms.

*(Ihr) lauft schnell = **Lauft** schnell!* Run fast!

The equivalent of the English **let's** form is simply the *wir* form with the verb first.

__Laufen wir__ schnell! Let's run fast!

The exclamation point in the imperative is particularly important in the *Sie* and *wir* forms of the written language because, other than context, that is the only thing that distinguishes it from a question. In the spoken language, the distinction is achieved through intonation.

Gehen Sie heute früh nach Hause? Are you going home early today?

Gehen Sie heute früh nach Hause! Go home early today.

Gehen wir heute früh nach Hause? Are we going home early today?

Gehen wir heute früh nach Hause! Let's go home early today.

6.4   The Use of the Future Tense *(das Futur)*

The future tense is used when there is nothing else in the sentence to indicate that the future is intended.

6.4.1   The Formation of the Future Tense

The future tense consists of the present tense of *werden* + infinitive.

*Ich **werde kommen**.* I will come.
*Du **wirst kommen**.* You will come.
*Er/Sie/Es **wird kommen**.* He/She/It will come.
*Wir **werden kommen**.* We will come.
*Ihr **werdet kommen**.* You will come.
*Sie **werden kommen**.* They will come.
*Sie **werden kommen**.* You will come.

28

The future tense of a modal has two infinitives.

*Ich **werde das machen müssen.*** I will have to do that.

6.5 The Use of the Simple Past Tense *(das Imperfekt)*

Except for *sein* and *haben* and the modals, the simple past tense (also called the narrative past) in German is used primarily in written rather than spoken German. For conversation, the present perfect tense is preferred. Just as in the present tense, in the simple past one verb form in German corresponds to three variations in English.

I **did** that.
I was **doing** that. } *Ich **machte** das.*
I **did do** that.

6.5.1 The Formation of the Simple Past Tense (Regular Verbs)

The simple past tense of regular verbs is formed by adding endings to the stem.

Ich machte das.	*Wir machten das.*
Du machtest das.	*Ihr machtet das.*
Sie machten das.	
Er/Sie/Es machte das.	*Sie machten das.*

Verbs like ***arbeiten,*** whose stems end in ***-d*** or ***-t,*** insert an ***-e-*** before the past-tense endings to aid pronunciation.

Ich arbeitete.	*Wir arbeiteten.*
Du arbeitetest.	*Ihr arbeitetet.*
Sie arbeiteten.	
Er/Sie/Es arbeitete.	*Sie arbeiteten.*

6.5.2 The Formation of the Simple Past Tense (Irregular Verbs)

Irregular verbs change the stem vowel and use the same endings as the present tense, except for first- and third-person singular, which have no ending.

Ich sah ihn.	*Wir sahen ihn.*
Du sahst ihn.	*Ihr saht ihn.*
	Sie sahen ihn.
Er/Sie/Es sah ihn.	*Sie sahen ihn.*

6.5.3 The Formation of the Simple Past Tense (Mixed Verbs)

Mixed verbs add an ending in the simple past tense (like regular verbs) and have a vowel change (like irregular verbs). Some of the most common are *bringen/brachte* (to bring), *denken/dachte* (to think), *kennen/kannte* (to know, to be acquainted with), and *wissen/ wußte* (to know a fact).

Ich kannte ihn gut. I knew him well.
Er wußte das schon. He knew that already.

6.5.4 The Formation of the Simple Past Tense (Modals)

Modals that have an umlaut in the infinitive drop the umlaut and add the past-tense endings.

Ich durfte nicht gehen. I wasn't allowed to go.
Du konntest nicht gehen. You weren't able to go.
Er mußte nicht gehen. He didn't have to go.
Wir sollten nicht gehen. We weren't supposed to go.
Ihr wolltet nicht gehen. You didn't want to go.
Sie mochten nicht gehen. * You didn't want to go.

* *Mögen* is rarely used in the simple past tense. The *g* of the stem changes to *ch*.

30

6.6 The Use of the Present Perfect Tense (das Perfekt)

The present perfect tense is used primarily in conversation. It refers to the same past time as the simple past and has the same meaning. The major exceptions are *sein, haben,* and *werden,* which are usually used in the simple past, even in conversation.

6.6.1 The Formation of the Present Perfect Tense

The present perfect tense consists of the present tense of *haben* or *sein* + the past participle.

6.6.2 The Formation of the Past Participle

The past participle of regular verbs adds a *ge-* prefix to the stem and the suffix *-t.*

Ich habe das gemacht. I did do that. I have done that.

The past participle of verbs whose stems end in *-d* or *-t* inserts an *-e-* just as in the simple past tense.

Er hat lange gearbeitet. He worked for a long time. He has worked for a long time. He did work for a long time.

The past participles of irregular verbs often have a vowel change and end in *-en* or *-n.* Their forms are not predictable and must be learned. Here are some of the most common.

gefunden	*finden*	to find
gegessen	*essen*	to eat
geheißen	*heißen*	to be called
geholfen	*helfen*	to help
gelesen	*lesen*	to read
genommen	*nehmen*	to take
geschlafen	*schlafen*	to sleep
geschrieben	*schreiben*	to write

31

gesehen	sehen	to see
gesprochen	sprechen	to speak
gesungen	singen	to sing
getragen	tragen	to carry/wear
getrunken	trinken	to drink
getan	tun to do	

The past participles of mixed verbs have a vowel change like irregular verbs and end in *-t* like regular verbs.

| gebracht | bringen | to bring |
| gedacht | denken | to think |

Two groups of verbs have no *ge-* prefix. The first consists of verbs with the inseparable prefixes *be-, emp-, ent-, er-, ge-, ver-, miß-,* or *zer-.*

Sie hat ein Bier bestellt. She ordered a beer.
Er hat mich empfohlen. He recommended me.

The other group consists of verbs that end in *-ieren.*

Wie lange hast du studiert? How long were you a student?
Er hat mir gratuliert. He congratulated me.

The past participle of the verb *sein* is irregular.

Bist du da gewesen? Were you there?

6.6.3   The Choice of the Auxiliary *haben* or *sein*

It might be easiest to learn *sein* along with the verbs requiring it. Since most verbs form the perfect tenses with *haben*, it is indicated in a dictionary when the auxiliary is *sein*. However, the choice can also be determined by asking these questions:

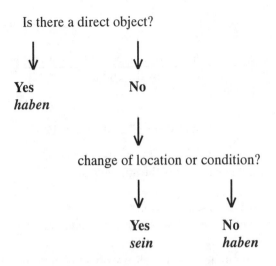

Is there a direct object?

↓   ↓

Yes   **No**
haben

                     ↓

change of location or condition?

              ↓   ↓

           Yes   **No**
           sein   *haben*

The present perfect of the verb *fahren* can illustrate the application of this process.

*Ich **bin** nach Hause gefahren.* I drove home.

Is there an accusative object? No. Is there a change of location or condition? Yes. Thus *sein* is used to form the present perfect tense.

*Ich **habe** sein Auto **gefahren**.* I drove his car.

Is there an accusative object? Yes. Thus ***haben*** is used.

Most verbs can only form the present perfect with **haben** OR **sein**, not both (as in the case of *fahren*).

The contrast between the verbs *schlafen* (to sleep) and *einschlafen* (to fall asleep) illustrates the point further.

*Er **hat** den ganzen Tag **geschlafen**.* He slept the whole day.

Is there a direct object? No. Is there a change of location or condition? No. The state of being asleep is described. Therefore, the auxiliary is ***haben***.

33

Er ist früh eingeschlafen. He fell asleep early.

Is there a direct object? No. Is there a change of location or condition? Yes. He was awake and he fell asleep. Therefore, the auxiliary is *sein.*

6.6.4   The Formation of the Present Perfect Tense (Modals)

Although it is possible to use modals in the present perfect tense, the preferred tense is the simple past.

*Ich **habe** das **gewollt**.*
Preferable: *Ich **wollte** das.* I wanted that.

When the modal is used with another verb in the present perfect tense, a double infinitive occurs.

*Ich **habe arbeiten wollen**.*
Preferable: *Ich **wollte arbeiten**.* I wanted to work.

6.7   The Use of the Past Perfect Tense (das Plusquamperfekt)

Once you have mastered the present perfect tense, the past perfect tense is a simple matter. It expresses a time further in the past than the simple past and the present perfect. Unlike the simple past and the present perfect, there is only one possible English equivalent for the German past perfect tense.

*Ich **hatte** das schon **getan**.* I **had** already **done** that.
*Er **war** schon **abgefahren**.* He **had** already **departed**.

6.7.1   The Formation of the Past Perfect Tense

Whereas the present perfect tense is formed with the present tense of ***haben*** or ***sein*** + the past participle, the past perfect tense is formed with the past tense of ***haben*** or ***sein*** + the past participle.

Wir hatten schon gegessen. We **had** already **eaten.**
Er war schon da gewesen. He **had** already **been** there.
Sie hatte das machen wollen.* She **had wanted to do** that.

* When the modal occurs in the past perfect tense, the double infinitive construction cannot be avoided.

6.8 Separable-Prefix Verbs

Many German verbs have a prefix that is separated from the verb in a main clause, in a question in the present and simple past tenses, and in the imperative. In the perfect tenses, the separable prefix comes before the *ge-* and the rest of the verb. Separable-prefix verbs can be recognized in the spoken language by the stress on the prefix. In the written language, the separable prefix generally has a meaning on its own, whereas a nonseparable prefix usually does not. The most common separable prefixes are *ab-, an-, auf-, aus-, ein-, her-, hin-, mit-, nach-, vor-, vorbei-, zu-,* and *zurück-.*

Die Studenten hören immer zu. The students always listen.
Die Studenten hörten immer zu. The students always listened.
Hören/Hörten die Studenten immer zu? Do/Did the students always listen?
Hören Sie zu! Listen.
Die Studenten haben immer zugehört. The students always listened.

35

CHAPTER 7

The Subjunctive
(Der Konjunktiv)

7.1 The Use of the General Subjunctive *(der Konjunktiv II)*

The general subjunctive is used to express ideas that are unreal or unlikely. In deciding whether or not to use it, one must decide whether or not the situation is real/likely (indicative) or unreal/unlikely (subjunctive).

Likely
Sie wird kommen, wenn sie kann. She will come, if she can. [indicative]

Unlikely
Sie würde kommen, wenn sie könnte. She would come, if she could. [subjunctive]

The general subjunctive is also used:

(a) when one wishes to be very polite or to express a request.

Würden Sie morgen bitte vorbeikommen? Would you please come by tomorrow?

(b) to express hypothetical statements and questions.

Was würden Sie machen, wenn Sie reich wären? What would you do if you were rich?

(c) to express a wish.

Wenn ich nur mehr Geld hätte! If only I had more money.

7.1.1 The Formation of the Present-Time General Subjunctive (Regular Verbs)

The general subjunctive of regular verbs derives its stem from the *wir* form of the simple past tense. It is formed by adding to the stem the dental suffix *-t* and the personal endings. For regular verbs, the general subjunctive is identical to the simple past tense.

ich arbeitete	*wir arbeiteten*
du arbeitetest	*ihr arbeitetet*
Sie arbeiteten	
er/sie/es arbeitete	*sie arbeiteten*

The subjunctive meaning is usually clear from the context.

Wir machten das. We did that.
Wir machten das. We would do that.

7.1.2 The Formation of the Present-Time General Subjunctive (Irregular Verbs)

The general subjunctive of irregular verbs also derives its stem from the *wir* form of the simple past tense. The personal endings are the same, but no dental suffix *-t-* occurs. In addition, irregular verbs with the vowels **a, o,** or **u** add an umlaut.

Wir kamen [simple past] + umlaut = Wir **kämen.** We would come.

7.1.3 The Formation of the Present-Time General Subjunctive (Modals)

Modals with an umlaut in the infinitive (all but *sollen* and *wollen*) also have an umlaut in the subjunctive. The present-time general subjunctive of *sollen* and *wollen* is thus identical to the simple past. Only the context makes the meaning clear.

Wir mußten schwer arbeiten. (simple past) We had to work hard.
Wir müßten schwer arbeiten. (subjunctive) We would have to work hard.
Wir sollten schwer arbeiten. (simple past and subjunctive) We were supposed to work hard./We should work hard.
Er sollte schwer arbeiten. (simple past and subjunctive) He was supposed to work hard./He should work hard.

7.1.4 *Würde* + Infinitive

Another form of the subjunctive can also be used for both regular and irregular verbs. It consists of the subjunctive form of *werden* + infinitive. This subjunctive is interchangeable with the other forms.

Wir machten das. = *Wir würden das machen.* We would do that.
Wir kämen. = *Wir würden kommen.* We would come.

In conversation, the first form, not the *würde* form, is preferred for the verbs *haben, sein,* and *wissen* and for the modals.

Wenn ich nur mehr Geld hätte! If only I had more money!
Wenn ich nur reich wäre! If only I were rich!
Wenn ich nur alles wüßte! If only I knew everything!
Wenn er wollte, könnte er kommen. If he wanted to, he could come.

38

7.2 The Use of the Past-Time General Subjunctive

Except for the fact that there are no polite requests in the past-time general subjunctive, the use is the same as that of the present-time general subjunctive. There is only one past tense in the subjunctive, so the past-time general subjunctive covers the simple past, the present perfect, and the past perfect of the indicative.

7.2.1 The Formation of the Past-Time General Subjunctive

The past-time general subjunctive is derived from the past perfect tense. It consists of the subjunctive form of the auxiliary *haben* or *sein* + the past participle.

Wir hätten das getan. We would have done that.
Er wäre gekommen. He would have come.

7.2.2 The Formation of the Past-Time General Subjunctive (Modals)

As is the case with the present and past perfect tenses of the indicative, the past-time subjunctive of modals has a double infinitive.

Wir hätten das machen sollen. We should have done that.
Er hätte kommen können. He could have come.

7.3 The Use of the Special Subjunctive (der Konjunktiv I)

The special subjunctive is rarely used except in newspapers, literature, and in literary and scientific essays. Nevertheless, one should be aware of and be able to recognize it. The special subjunctive is used in indirect discourse to convey the thoughts and opinions of someone else. It absolves the person reporting from any responsibility by making it clear that the thoughts expressed are those of another person. It does not express contrary-to-fact conditions or wishes.

7.3.1 The Formation of the Special Subjunctive

Whereas the **general subjunctive** is based on the **simple past tense** of the *wir* form of the verb, the **special subjunctive** is based upon the **present tense** of that verb form. It has the same endings as the general subjunctive. Note that in German, just as in English, the pronoun often changes in indirect discourse and that the tense of the introductory statement has no effect on the tense of the indirect statement. The forms of the third-person singular are the ones most frequently used because they differ from the indicative forms.

*Sie sagte, sie **werde kommen,** wenn sie **könne.*** She said she'll come if she can.

*Er fragte, ob ich morgen wieder **vorbeikomme***/**vorbeikäme.*** He asked if I'll come by again tomorrow.

*Ich sagte, wir **haben***/**hätten** das **gemacht.*** I said we did that.

*Er sagt, wir **müssen***/**müßten** schwer arbeiten.* He says we have to work hard.

*Sie sagte, er **solle** schwer arbeiten.* She said he should work hard.

*Sie sagte, er **habe** schwer **arbeiten sollen.*** She said he should have worked hard.

*   When the special subjunctive form is the same as the indicative forms, the general subjunctive is preferred.

The special subjunctive of the verb *sein* is irregular.

ich sei	*wir seien*
du seiest	*ihr seiet*
Sie seien	
er/sie/es sei	*sie seien*

40

CHAPTER 8

The Passive Voice
(Das Passiv)

8.1 The Use of the Passive Voice

In German as in English, the active voice is used more frequently than the passive voice. In the active voice, the subject is active and performs an action.

ACTIVE
Der Hausmeister schließt das Fenster. The janitor **closes** the window.

In the passive voice, the subject is passive and is not performing an action, but is acted upon.

PASSIVE
Das Fenster wird vom Hausmeister geschlossen. The window **is closed** by the janitor.

The passive voice shifts the emphasis from the performer to the recipient of the action. As the examples above illustrate, the direct object of the active sentence *(das Fenster)* becomes the subject of the passive sentence.

It is important to remember that the passive is always used to describe an action and not a state. Do not confuse it with constructions involving the verb *sein* (to be) and a past participle used as a predicate adjective.

*Das Fenster **ist geschlossen.*** The window **is closed.** (active — describes a state)
*Das Fenster **wird** jeden Tag um 5 Uhr **geschlossen.*** The window is closed every day at 5 o'clock. (passive — describes an action)

Notice that in the English examples above there is no difference in construction between the passive form and the form describing a state. In German, in contrast, the passive form differs from the active form; this often causes problems for English speakers learning the passive in German.

8.1.1   The Formation of the Present Tense of the Passive Voice

All tenses of the passive voice in German consist of a form of the verb *werden* and a **past participle.** The present tense of the passive consists of **the present tense of** *werden* + **past participle.**

In the passive, the agent (the person or thing performing the action) is often omitted, but when it is included, the preposition *von* is used when the agent is a person, and the preposition *durch* when the agent is impersonal and the meaning is "as a result of" or "by means of."

*Das Fenster **wird vom Hausmeister geschlossen.*** The window is closed by the janitor.
*Das Fenster **wird durch** den Wind **geschlossen.*** The window is closed by the wind.

8.1.2   The Formation of the Simple Past Tense of the Passive Voice

The simple past tense of the passive consists of the simple past of *werden* + **past participle.**

*Das Fenster **wurde** vom Hausmeister **geschlossen**.* The window was closed by the janitor.

8.1.3   The Formation of the Present Perfect Tense of the Passive Voice

The present perfect tense of the passive consists of the present tense of *sein* + **past participle** + *worden*.

*Das Fenster **ist** vom Hausmeister **geschlossen worden**.* The window was/has been closed by the janitor.

Worden is a form that appears only in the perfect tenses of the passive. The perfect tenses of the passive are always formed with the verb *sein*, never with *haben*.

8.1.4   The Formation of the Past Perfect Tense of the Passive Voice

The past perfect tense of the passive consists of the simple past of *sein* + **past participle** + *worden*.

*Das Fenster **war** vom Hausmeister **geschlossen worden**.* The window had been closed by the janitor.

8.1.5   The Formation of the Future Tense of the Passive Voice

The future tense of the passive consists of the present tense of *werden* + **past participle** + *werden*.

*Das Fenster **wird** vom Hausmeister **geschlossen werden**.* The window will be closed by the janitor.

8.1.6   Modals in the Passive Voice

Modals are rarely used in the passive voice in tenses other than the present and the simple past. The present usually covers the future as well, and the simple past takes care of all past tenses.

The present passive with a modal consists of the present tense of the **modal + past participle + *werden.***

Das Fenster soll geschlossen werden. The window should be closed.

The simple past passive with a modal consists of the simple past of the **modal + past participle + *werden.***

Das Fenster sollte geschlossen werden. The window was supposed to have been closed.

8.2 Verbs with Dative Objects in the Passive Voice

Verbs that take only a dative object must retain the dative object in the passive. Since there is no accusative object in the active sentence, such sentences have no grammatical subject in the German passive. *Es* is the understood subject. Therefore, the verb is always in the third-person singular, even though the subject in the English equivalent is plural.

ACTIVE
Freunde helfen ihnen oft. Friends often help them.

PASSIVE
Ihnen wird oft von Freunden geholfen. They are often helped by friends.

8.3 Other Verbs with No Object in the Passive Voice

Some verbs, such as *arbeiten* and *lachen,* have no object in the active voice. Others can omit the object in the active voice. These verbs can form passives to express an activity. They have no grammatical subject and the verb is always in the third-person singular.

*Hier **wird** immer viel **gearbeitet.*** There is always a lot of work done here.

*Bei uns **wird** immer gut **gegessen.*** At our house, there is always good eating.

Sometimes these constructions use *es* as a syntactical filler, but the meaning is the same.

Es wird** hier immer viel **gearbeitet.
Es wird** bei uns immer gut **gegessen.

8.4 Passive Substitutes

Several methods are commonly used to avoid the passive altogether in German. The most common is the use of *man* (one, a person, you, they).

*Hier **spricht man** Deutsch. = Hier wird Deutsch gesprochen.* German is spoken here.

Another possibility is the use of *sich lassen* + infinitive.

*Das **läßt sich machen**. = Das kann gemacht werden.* That can be done.

Sein + *zu* + infinitive is often used in place of a passive construction with a modal.

*Das Auto **ist** heute noch **zu reparieren**. = Das Auto muß heute noch repariert werden.* The car must still be repaired today.

CHAPTER 9

Interrogatives

9.1 About Questions in General

There are three ways to form questions in German.

(a) To form general questions without interrogatives, simply **invert subject and verb.**

> *Kommt er heute?* Is he coming today?
> *Sieht sie ihn?* Does she see him?

(b) More specific questions use interrogatives. Note that in these questions the subject and verb are also inverted.

> *Wann kommt er?* When is he coming?
> *Warum/Wieso kommt er?* Why is he coming?
> *Wie lange bleibt er?* How long is he staying?
> *Was hat er gesagt?* What did he say?
> *Wie alt ist er?* How old is he?
> *Wieviele Kinder hat er?* How many children does he have?
> *Wieviel/Was kostet das?* How much does that cost?
> *Was für ein Mann ist er?* What kind of a man is he?
> *Was für einen Wagen hat er?* What kind of a car does he have?

Note that the case of the noun following *was für* is determined by its use in the sentence. In the first example with *was für* above, *ein Mann* is nominative because of the verb *sein*. In the second example, *einen Wagen* is accusative because it is the direct object of the verb *haben*.

When an interrogative is used in an indirect statement, it functions as a subordinating conjunction and the conjugated verb goes to the end of the clause it introduces.

> *Ich weiß nicht, wann er kommt.* I don't know when he is coming.
> *Hat er gesagt, wieviel das kostet?* Did he say how much that costs?

(c) A question can also be formed by simply adding *nicht wahr?* to the end of a statement.

> *Er kommt heute, nicht wahr?* He's coming today, isn't he?
> *Er hat einen VW, nicht wahr?* He has a VW, doesn't he?

9.2   The Interrogative *Wer?* (Who?)

The form of the German interrogative *wer?* (who) depends upon its case.

NOMINATIVE
Wer ist das? Who is that?

ACCUSATIVE
Wen hast du gesehen? Who did you see?

DATIVE
Wem gibt er das Buch? To whom is he giving the book?

GENITIVE
Wessen Buch ist das? Whose book is that?

9.3 The Interrogatives *Wo?*, *Woher?*, and *Wohin?* (Where?)

German has three words that correspond to the English "where?".

(a) *Wo?* simply asks about location.

> *Wo wohnt er?* Where does he live?
> *Wo liegt Essen?* Where is Essen situated?

(b) *Wohin?* (literally, where to?) is used only with verbs of motion, and indicates motion **away from** the speaker to another location.

> *Wohin geht er?* Where is he going?

(c) *Woher?* (from where?) is also used only with verbs of motion; it indicates motion from another location **toward** the speaker.

> *Woher kommt er?* Where does he come from?

9.4 The Interrogative *Welcher?* (Which?)

The interrogative *welcher?* is declined exactly like the definite article.

> *Welcher Mann kommt?* Which man is coming?
> *Welchen Mann siehst du?* Which man do you see?
> *Welches Buch liest du?* Which book are you reading?
> *Welche Frau kommt?* Which woman is coming?
> *In welchem Haus wohnt sie?* In which house does she live?

CHAPTER 10

Prepositions

10.1 About Prepositions in General

Prepositions are problematic in any language because they can have many meanings, both literal and figurative, and are often idiomatic. When learning German prepositions and their meanings, one should also learn which case follows the preposition. Some prepositions are always followed by an accusative object, some by a dative object, and others by a genitive object. Some can have either a dative or an accusative object. In addition, certain verb and preposition combinations should be learned together.

10.2 Prepositions with the Accusative Case

Five prepositions are always followed by the accusative case: *durch* (through), *für* (for), *gegen* (against), *ohne* (without), *um* (around, at).

Wir fuhren durch die Stadt. We drove through the city.
Ich habe etwas für dich. I have something for you.
Was hat er gegen mich? What does he have against me?
Sie kamen ohne die Kinder. They came without the children.
Der Hund läuft um den Wagen. The dog is running around the car.

*Sie kommen **um 3 Uhr an.*** They are arriving at 3 o'clock.

10.3   Prepositions with the Dative Case

The following prepositions are always followed by the dative case: ***aus*** (out of, from), ***außer*** (besides, except for), ***bei*** (at/for, near, at the home of), ***mit*** (with, by means of), ***nach*** (after, to [a city or country]), ***seit*** (since, for [with time expressions]), ***von*** (of, from, by), ***zu*** (to).

*Er kommt **aus dem Haus.*** He is coming out of the house.
*Sie kommen **aus Berlin.*** They are from Berlin.
***Außer mir** war niemand dort.* Except for me, no one was there.
*Er arbeitet **bei VW.*** He works for VW.
*Die Drogerie ist **bei der Tankstelle.*** The drug store is near the gas station.
*Sie wohnt **bei uns.*** She is living at our home.
*Kommt er **mit uns?*** Is he coming with us?
*Er fährt **mit dem Zug.*** He is traveling by train.
*Was machst du **nach der Arbeit?*** What are you doing after work?
*Wir fliegen **nach Berlin.*** We are flying to Berlin.
*Wir arbeiten **seit dem 4. Juni** hier.* We have been working here since June 4th.
*Wir wohnen **seit drei Jahren** dort.* We have been living there for three years.
*Ist sie eine Freundin **von dir?*** Is she a friend of yours?
*Er arbeitete **von Januar** bis Mai dort.* He worked there from January to May.
***Von wem** ist der Roman?* Who is the novel by?
*Gehst du jetzt **zum Bahnhof?*** Are you going to the train station now?

10.4   Prepositions with the Genitive Case

Four prepositions take the genitive case, although the dative is frequently used in colloquial speech: *(an)statt* (instead of), ***trotz*** (in spite of), ***während*** (during), ***wegen*** (because of).

(An)statt des Weines trinke ich das Bier. Instead of the wine I'll drink the beer.

Trotz des Wetters gehen wir heute schwimmen. Despite the weather we are going swimming today.

Während der Woche habe ich wenig Zeit. During the week I have little time.

Wegen des Wetters gehen wir heute nicht schwimmen. Because of the weather, we aren't going swimming today.

10.5 Prepositions with Either the Dative or the Accusative Case

The following prepositions can be followed either by a dative or an accusative object: *an* (on, at), *auf* (on, upon, on top of), *hinter* (behind, in back of), *in* (in, into, inside of), *neben* (next to, beside), *über* (over, above, across), *unter* (under, among), *vor* (in front of, before), *zwischen* (between). If the prepositional phrase simply describes location, that is, answers the question "where?" *(wo?)* — the **dative** is used. If it describes motion toward a destination (not just motion), that is, answers the question "where to?" *(wohin?)* — the **accusative** is used.

Das Buch liegt auf dem Tisch. The book is lying on the table.
   wo? = dative

Er legt das Buch auf den Tisch. He places the book on the table.
   wohin? = accusative

Das Bild hängt an der Wand. The picture is hanging on the wall.
   wo? = dative

Ich hänge das Bild an die Wand. I am hanging the picture on the wall. *wohin?* = accusative

Wir arbeiten hinter dem Haus. We are working behind the house.
   wo? = dative

Wir gingen hinter das Haus. We went behind the house.
   wohin? = accusative

Ich esse gern in diesem Restaurant. I like eating in this restaurant. *wo?* = dative

Ich gehe gern in dieses Restaurant. I like going to this restaurant. *wohin?* = accusative

Sie saß neben mir gestern abend. She sat next to me last night.
wo? = dative

Sie setzte sich neben mich. She seated herself next to me.
wohin? = accusative

Die Lampe hängt über dem Tisch. The lamp is hanging over the table. *wo?* = dative

Sie hängte die Lampe über den Tisch. She hung the lamp over the table. *wohin?* = accusative

Wir gingen über die Straße. We went across the street.
wohin? = accusative

Der Hund liegt unter dem Tisch. The dog is lying under the table. *wo?* = dative

Der Ball rollt unter den Tisch. The ball rolled under the table.
wohin? = accusative

Das Auto steht vor dem Haus. The car is in front of the house.
wo? = dative

Er fuhr das Auto vor das Haus. He drove the car up in front of the house. *wohin?* = accusative

Mein Wagen steht zwischen dem grünen und dem blauen Auto.
My car is standing between the green and the blue car.
wo? = dative

Ich fuhr meinen Wagen zwischen das grüne und das blaue Auto.
I drove my car between the green and the blue car.
wohin? = accusative

10.6 Some Idiomatic and Other Uses of Prepositions

an (at)

Wie lange studiert er an der Universität? How long has he been studying at the university?

auf (in, to)

Sie wohnen auf dem Land. They live in the country.
Wir fahren oft auf das Land. We often drive to the country.

aus (out of, of, for, made out of)
   Sie tat es aus Angst. She did it out of fear.
   Sein Haus ist aus Holz. His house is made of wood.

außer (out of, beside [himself, etc.])
   Die Maschine ist außer Betrieb. The machine is out of order.
   Wir waren alle außer Atem. We were all out of breath.
   Er war außer sich. He was beside himself.

bei (with, by/in the process of, whenever/in the case of)
   Du hast nie Geld bei dir. You never have money with you.
   Beim Sprechen macht er viele Fehler. In the process of speaking, he makes lots of mistakes.
   Bei schönem Wetter machen wir einen Spaziergang. Whenever the weather is nice, we take a walk.

bis in (into) *bis an* (right up to)
   Wir feierten bis in die Nacht. We celebrated into the night.
   Wir fuhren bis an seine Tür. We drove right up to his door.

durch (by means of, through)
   Wir haben uns durch Zufall kennengelernt. We met by chance.
   Er hat seine Frau durch Freunde kennengelernt. He met his wife through friends.

für (for, by)
   Er kennt das Gedicht Wort für Wort. He knows the poem word for word.
   Man muß das Schritt für Schritt machen. One must do that step by step.

gegen (around, about)
   Wir waren gegen 6 Uhr zu Hause. We were home around 6 o'clock.

in (to, at, on)

*Wann geht sie **in die Schule?*** When does she go to school?

*Sie ist schon **in der Schule**.* She is already at school.

*Ich gehe gern **ins Konzert**.* I like going to a concert.

*Wir wohnen **im dritten Stock**.* We live on the third floor.

nach (in, according to)

***Meiner Meinung nach** soll er länger daran arbeiten.* In my opinion, he should work on that longer.

***Diesem Buch nach** war er jahrelang Minister.* According to this book, he was a minister for years.

Note that ***nach*** follows its object when it corresponds to English "according to."

unter (beneath, between, under the influence of)

*Das ist **unter seiner Würde**.* That is beneath his dignity.

***Unter uns** gesagt, versteht er das nicht.* Just between us, he doesn't understand that.

***Unter dem Einfluß von** Alkohol darf man **nicht** Auto fahren.* One is not allowed to drive a car under the influence of alcohol.

zu (at, by, for)

*Wo seid ihr **zu Weihnachten?*** Where will you be at Christmas?

*Ich bin heute abend **zu Hause**.* I will be at home this evening.

*Gehst du oft **zu Fuß?*** Do you often go by foot?

*Er ist jetzt **zum dritten Mal** in Frankreich.* He is now in France for the third time.

*Was hast du **zum Geburtstag** bekommen?* What did you receive for your birthday?

10.7 Contractions

The following contractions of prepositions and the definite article are possible:

an das = **ans**	*bei dem* = **beim**	*von dem* = **vom**	*zu dem* = **zum**
an dem = **am**	*in das* = **ins**	*vor das* = **vors**	*zu der* = **zur**
auf das = **aufs**	*in dem* = **im**	*vor dem* = **vorm**	

10.8 Common Verb-Preposition Combinations

In verb-preposition combinations, the preposition must be followed by an object in the appropriate case. Prepositions that can be followed by either the dative or the accusative usually take the accusative.

Do not confuse verb-preposition combinations with separable-prefix verbs. In the case of separable prefixes, the prefix goes to the end of a main clause and is followed by nothing.

denken an [+ acc.] to think of
Ich denke oft an dich. I think of you often.

schreiben an [+ acc.] to write to
Du mußt an deine Eltern schreiben. You must write to your parents.

sich freuen auf [+ acc.] to look forward to
Er freut sich auf seine Reise. He is looking forward to his trip.

warten auf [+ acc.] to wait for
Wartest du auf mich? Are you waiting for me?

sich interessieren für [+ acc.] to be interested in
Sie interessiert sich für moderne Musik. She is interested in modern music.

sich ärgern über [+ acc.] to be annoyed about
Wir ärgern uns über unsere Arbeit. We are annoyed about our work.

erzählen von [+ dat.] to tell about
Ich erzählte von meiner Reise. I told about my trip.

halten von [+ dat.] to think about
Was hältst du von dem Roman? What do you think about the
   novel?

sprechen von [+ dat.] to talk about
Wir haben von dem Konzert gesprochen. We talked about the
   concert.

CHAPTER 11

Adjectives

11.1 About Adjectives in General

There are two basic kinds of adjectives: predicate and attributive adjectives. **Predicate adjectives** occur after the verb and do not precede a noun.

Er ist interessant. He is **interesting.**

Attributive adjectives precede a noun.

*Er ist ein **interessanter** Mann.* He is an **interesting** man.

As these examples illustrate, there is no difference in English in the form of predicate and attributive adjectives, whereas there is in German. In German, predicate adjectives have no ending *(interessant),* but attributive adjectives do *(interessanter).*

11.2 Unpreceded Adjective Endings

The endings of adjectives that are not preceded by a definite or an indefinite article are the easiest to learn. With two exceptions (masculine and neuter genitive singular), they are the same as the ending of the definite article. Below is a comparison of unpreceded adjective endings, (in parentheses) with the definite article.

	Masculine	Feminine	Neuter	Plural
Nominative	der (-er)	die (-e)	das (-es)	die (-e)
Accusative	den (-en)	die (-e)	das (-es)	die (-e)
Dative	dem (-em)	der (-er)	dem (-em)	den (-en)
Genitive	des (-en)	der (-er)	des (-en)	der (-er)

Guter Wein ist teuer (der). Good wine is expensive.
Er kauft immer teuren Wein (den). He always buys expensive wine.
Ich esse gern frisches Obst (das). I like eating fresh fruit.
Wegen schlechten Wetters blieben wir zu Hause (des). Because of bad weather, we stayed at home.

11.3   Preceded Adjective Endings

The most commonly occurring attributive adjective ending when preceded by an "*ein*-word" or a "*der*-word" is -*en;* of the 32 possible endings for preceded adjectives, 22 are -*en,* (illustrated in the charts in the next two sections). Thus, if in doubt, guess -*en.* Just think of the endings that are not -*en* as exceptions to the general rule that preceded attributive adjectives end in -*en.*

11.3.1   Adjective Endings After *der*-Words

The following endings occur after "*der*-words" *(der, dieser, jeder, mancher, solcher, welcher):*

	Masculine	Feminine	Neuter	Plural
Nominative	-e	-e	-e	-en
Accusative	-en	-e	-e	-en
Dative	-en	-en	-en	-en
Genitive	-en	-en	-en	-en

The sentence below contains all of the exceptions to the general rule that attributive adjectives end in -*en.*

58

Der dicke Mann, die schlanke Frau und das schreiende Kind essen die heiße Wurst und trinken das kalte Bier. The fat man, the slender woman, and the screaming child are eating the hot sausage and drinking the cold beer.

Note that the exceptions are limited to the nominative (all genders) and accusative (feminine and neuter) cases. They are all singular.

11.3.2 Adjective Endings After *ein*-Words

The following endings occur after "*ein*-words" (*ein, kein,* and the possessive adjectives):

	Masculine	Feminine	Neuter	Plural
Nominative	*-er*	*-e*	*-es*	*-en*
Accusative	*-en*	*-e*	*-es*	*-en*
Dative	*-en*	*-en*	*-en*	*-en*
Genitive	*-en*	*-en*	*-en*	*-en*

Note that, as with "*der*-words," the exceptions are again all singular and occur in the nominative (all genders) and accusative (feminine and neuter) cases.

Ein dicker Mann, eine schlanke Frau und ein schreiendes Kind essen eine heiße Wurst und trinken ein kaltes Bier.

11.4 Comparison of Adjectives and Adverbs

In both English and German, adjectives can have three forms.

Positive	Comparative	Superlative
nett	*netter*	*nettest-*
(nice)	(nicer)	(nicest)
intelligent	*intelligenter*	*intelligentest-*
(intelligent)	(more intelligent)	(most intelligent)

As these examples indicate, the formation of the comparative and superlative in German is easier than in English. There is only one way to form the comparative and superlative in German, whereas English sometimes adds an ending (cold/colder) and sometimes forms the comparative with "more" (more expensive).

11.4.1 Formation of the Comparative and Superlative

In the comparative, adjectives add an *-er.* In the superlative, they add an *-(e)st.* The *-e* is inserted for most adjectives ending in *-d, -t,* or an *s*-sound. In addition, most one-syllable adjectives with the vowels *a, o,* or *u* add an umlaut.

Positive	Comparative	Superlative
alt	*älter*	*ältest-*
jung	*jünger*	*jüngst-*
kalt	*kälter*	*kältest-*
warm	*wärmer*	*wärmst-*

11.4.2 Attributive Adjectives in the Comparative and Superlative

The comparative can occur as either a **predicate adjective** or an **attributive adjective.**

Predicate adjective
Mein Auto ist neu, aber seins ist neuer. My car is new, but his is newer.

Attributive adjective
Er hat ein neueres Auto als ich. He has a newer car than I.

Note in the example above that the comparative attributive adjective *neueres* first adds the comparative ending *(-er)* and then the adjective ending *(-es).*

Just as in English, German superlative forms are preceded by the definite article or a possessive adjective (**the/my oldest, the/her youngest, the/our coldest, the/his warmest**). Therefore, they are attributive adjectives and must have an adjective ending, which is added after the superlative ending has been added.

> *Sein Auto ist **das neueste** Auto hier.* His car is the newest car here.

11.4.3 The Superlative Predicate Adjective/Adverb

There is an alternate form for the superlative predicate adjective or adverb. It always follows this pattern: ***am*** + (adjective or adverb) + ***-sten***.

> *Mein Auto ist neu, aber sein Auto ist **am neuesten**.* My car is new, but his car is the newest.

11.5 Irregular Forms in the Comparative and Superlative

gern	*lieber*	*liebst-*	(see examples below)
groß	*größer*	*größt-*	(big, bigger, biggest)
gut	*besser*	*best-*	(good, better, best)
hoch	*höher*	*höchst-*	(high, higher, highest)
nah	*näher*	*nächst-*	(near, nearer, nearest)
viel	*mehr*	*meist-*	(much, more, most)

Ich sehe gern fern. I **like** watching TV.
Ich arbeite lieber im Garten. I **prefer** working in the yard.
Am liebsten lese ich ein Buch. I **like** reading a book **best of all**.

11.6 Special Phrases Used in Comparisons

(a) *(genau) so… wie* and *nicht so… wie* are used to say that one thing is, or is not, like another.

> *Sein Auto ist **genau so** neu **wie** meins.* His car is just as new as mine.
> *Sein Auto ist **nicht so** schön **wie** meins.* His car isn't as beautiful as mine.

(b) *als* is used to compare two things of different value.

>*Mein Auto ist schöner als seins.* My car is more beautiful than his.

(c) *immer* + comparative is used to express the idea that something is continually becoming more and more so.

>*Wir werden immer reicher.* We are getting richer and richer.

(d) *je* + comparative ... *desto* + comparative is used with two comparatives.

>*Je reicher wir werden, desto weniger arbeiten wir.* The richer we become, the less we work.

11.7 Adjectival Nouns

Some nouns in German are derived from adjectives and have adjective endings. Some of the most common are *der Deutsche, der Angestellte* (employee), *der Bekannte* (acquaintance), *der Kranke* (the sick person), *der Verlobte* (fiancé), *der Verwandte* (relative). These adjectival nouns are capitalized, but they follow the rules for adjective endings, according to whether they are preceded by the definite article, indefinite article, or no article.

Der Verwandte war bei ihm. The relative was with him.
Ein Verwandter war bei ihm. A relative was with him.
Die Verwandten waren bei ihm. The relatives were with him.
Verwandte kommen oft zu ihm. Relatives often come to him.

CHAPTER 12

Word Order

12.1 About Word Order in General

The most general and basic rule of German word order is that
the conjugated verb comes in second place. The first element can
be any of the following things:

(a) the subject

> *Der Hund beißt den Mann.* The dog bites the man.

(b) an object

> *Den Mann beißt der Hund.* The dog bites the man.

(c) an interrogative

> *Was macht der Hund?* What is the dog doing?

(d) an adverb

> *Gestern hat der Hund den Mann gebissen.* The dog bit the
> man yesterday.

(e) or an entire phrase

Als ich gestern vorbeiging, **hat** *der Hund den Mann gebissen.*
As I walked by yesterday, the dog bit the man.

In only three instances does the verb come first.

(a) in a general question

Beißt *der Hund den Mann?* Does the dog bite the man?

(b) in a command

Bleiben *Sie still!* Stay still!

(c) to express an if-clause

Bliebe *der Mann still, würde der Hund ihn nicht beißen.* If
the man would remain still, the dog wouldn't bite him.

12.2 Coordinating Conjunctions

Coordinating conjunctions join two independent clauses. They
do **not** affect word order: in both clauses, the verb remains in second
place. The coordinating conjunctions are *aber* (but), *denn* (because,
for), *oder* (or), *sondern* (but, rather, on the contrary), and *und* (and).
Sondern rather than *aber* is used to connect a negative clause to a
correction in the following clause.

Der Hund **beißt** *den Mann,* **aber** *es* **tut** *nicht weh.* The dog bites
the man, but it doesn't hurt.
Der Mann **muß** *still bleiben,* **oder** *der Hund* **wird** *ihn beißen.*
The man must stay still, or the dog will bite him.
Der Hund **beißt** *den Mann,* **denn** *er* **bleibt** *nicht still.* The dog
bites the man, because he doesn't stay still.
Der Mann **bleibt** *nicht still,* **und** *der Hund* **beißt** *ihn.* The man
doesn't stay still, and the dog bites him.

Der Mann bleibt nicht still, sondern (er) läuft weg. The man doesn't stay still, but rather runs away.

Note that coordinating conjunctions in German are set off by a comma.

12.3   Subordinating Conjunctions

Subordinating conjunctions join an independent and a dependent (subordinate) clause. A subordinate clause is a clause that cannot stand alone as a complete sentence. In a clause introduced by a subordinating conjunction, the conjugated verb is pushed to the end of the clause. A subordinate clause is always set off by a comma.

Here are the most common subordinating conjunctions.

als when	*ob* whether, if
bevor before	*obwohl* although
bis until	*seitdem* since [temporal]
da because	*sobald* as soon as
damit so that, in order that	*solange* as long as
daß that	*während* while
ehe before	*weil* because
falls in case	*wenn* if,when/whenever
nachdem after	

Als der Mann noch still war, hat der Hund ihn nicht gebissen.
When the man was still quiet, the dog didn't bite him.
Bevor der Hund ihn gebissen hat, hat der Mann sich bewegt.
Before the dog bit him, the man moved.
Der Hund hat ihn nicht gebissen, bis er sich bewegt hat. The dog didn't bite him until he moved.
Der Hund hat ihn gebissen, da (weil) er sich bewegt hat. The dog bit him because he moved.
Der Mann blieb still, damit der Hund ihn nicht beißen würde. The man remained still so that the dog wouldn't bite him.
Er wußte, daß der Hund ihn beißen würde. He knew that the dog would bite him.

Ehe der Hund ihn gebissen hat, hat der mann sich bewegt. Before the dog bit him, the man moved.

Der Mann blieb still, falls der Hund ihn beißen könnte. The man remained still in case the dog might/could bite him.

Nachdem der Hund ihn gebissen hatte, fuhr man ihn ins Krankenhaus. After the dog had bitten him, he was driven to the hospital.

Ich weiß nicht, ob es weh tat. I don't know if it hurt.

Obwohl der Hund ihn gebissen hatte, konnte der Mann noch gehen. Although the dog had bitten him, the man could still walk.

Seitdem der Hund ihn gebissen hat, hat er Angst vor Hunden. Since the dog bit him he has been afraid of dogs.

Sobald er im Krankenhaus war, ging es ihm besser. As soon as he was in the hospital, he was better.

Solange er still blieb, hat der Hund ihn nicht gebissen. As long as he remained still, the dog didn't bit him.

Während er im Krankenhaus war, ließ er sich untersuchen. While he was in the hospital, he had himself examined.

Weil (Da) der Hund ihn gebissen hat, hat er Hunde nicht gern. Because the dog bit him, he doesn't like dogs.

Wenn ein Hund Sie gebissen hätte, hätten Sie Hunde auch nicht gern. If a dog had bitten you, you would also not like dogs.

Wenn er einen Hund sieht, möchte er am liebsten weglaufen. When/Whenever he sees a dog, he would prefer to run away.

12.3.1 Interrogatives in a Subordinate Clause

Interrogatives may also be used to introduce a subordinate clause that is an indirect question.

Ich weiß nicht, warum der Hund ihn gebissen hat. I don't know why the dog bit him.

Er wußte nicht, wem der Hund gehört. He didn't know who the dog belongs to.

12.3.2 Modals in a Subordinate Clause

When a modal occurs with a dependent infinitive in a subordinate clause, the modal, as the conjugated verb, goes to the end of the clause.

> *Der Arzt sagte, daß der Mann nach Hause* **gehen dürfte.** The doctor said that the man was allowed to go home.

When there is a double infinitive, the modal does not go all the way to the end of the subordinate clause, but just before the double infinitive.

> *Der Arzt sagte, daß der Mann* **hätte weglaufen sollen.** The doctor said that the man should have run away.

12.3.3 Separable-Prefix Verbs in a Subordinate Clause

Separable-prefix verbs are reunited with their prefix at the end of a subordinate clause and are written as one word.

> *Als der Mann im Krankenhaus* **ankam,** *war seine Frau schon da.* When the man arrived at the hospital, his wife was already there.

12.4 Time, Manner, Place

Another basic rule of German word order is that adverbs of time come first, followed next by those of manner, and finally those of place.

TIME	MANNER	PLACE
Heute fahre ich	*mit dem Wagen*	*nach Berlin.*

Today I am going by car to Berlin.

If two time expressions occur together, the more general one precedes the more specific one.

> *Er ist* **heute um 3 Uhr** *abgefahren.* He left today at 3 o'clock.

12.5   The Position of Objects

The position of objects is somewhat complicated in the abstract. It might be easier to memorize the simple examples below than to learn the rules that follow.

Examples

Ich gebe dem Mann ein Buch. I am giving the man a book.

Rule: When there are two noun objects, the **indirect object** comes **before** the **direct object.**

Ich gebe ihm ein Buch. I am giving him a book.
Ich gebe es dem Mann. I am giving it to the man.

Rule: When there is a **pronoun object** and a **noun object,** the pronoun object comes **first.**

Ich gebe es ihm. I am giving it to him.

Rule: When there are **two pronoun objects,** the **direct object** comes **before** the **indirect object.**

12.6   The Position of *Nicht*

Generally, *nicht* comes after the subject and verb, objects, and time expressions. Thus it is often at the end of the sentence before any infinitive.

Der Hund wird den Mann morgen nicht beißen. The dog won't bite the man tomorrow.

CHAPTER 13

Special Problems

13.1 *Als, Wenn, Wann*

Als, wenn, and *wann* all correspond to English "when."

Als is used in statements about one past event.

Als ich vor kurzem mit ihm sprach, war er freundlich. When I talked to him a short time ago, he was friendly.

Wenn corresponds to English "whenever" (recurrence) and often implies the future.

Wenn ich mit ihm spreche, ist er freundlich. When/Whenever I talk to him, he is friendly.

Wann is used only in questions, direct and indirect.

Wann fängt die Vorstellung an? When does the performance begin?
Ich weiß nicht, wann die Vorstellung anfängt. I don't know when the performance begins.

13.2 *Nachdem, Nach, Nachher*

Nachdem (after) is a subordinating conjunction. It is used only with the present perfect or past perfect tenses.

> *Nachdem ich mit ihm gesprochen hatte, war er freundlich.* After I had talked to him, he was friendly.

Nach (after) is a preposition.

> *Nach dem Gespräch war er freundlich.* After the conversation, he was friendly.

Nachher (afterwards) is an adverb of time.

> *Gestern gingen wir ins Kino. Nachher haben wir gegessen.* Yesterday we went to the movies. Afterwards, we ate.

13.3 *Seitdem, Seit*

Seitdem (since) is a subordinating conjunction.

> *Seitdem ich mit ihm arbeite, ist er freundlich.* Since I have been working with him, he has been friendly.

Seitdem is also an adverb meaning "since then."

> *Ich habe neulich mit ihm gesprochen. Seitdem ist er nett zu mir.* I spoke to him recently. Since then he has been nice to me.)

Seit (for, since) is a preposition used in time expressions. It does not express a causal relationship.

> *Ich arbeite mit ihm seit drei Monaten.* I have been working with him for three months.

13.4 *Bevor, Vor, Vorher*

Bevor (before) is a subordinating conjunction.

Bevor ich mit ihm sprach, war er unfreundlich. Before I spoke to him, he was unfriendly.

Vor (before, in front of) is a preposition.

Er stand vor meinem Haus. He was standing in front of my house.

With time expressions, *vor* corresponds to English "ago."

Das war vor drei Monaten. That was three months ago.

Vorher (before that) is an adverb of time.

Ich habe neulich mit ihm gesprochen und er war nett. Vorher war er nicht nett. I spoke to him recently and he was nice. Before that, he was not nice.

13.5 *Noch Ein, Ein Ander-*

Noch ein is used to ask for an additional one of something that one has.

*Herr Ober, **noch ein** Bier bitte!* Waiter, another beer please.

Ein ander- is used to obtain a different version of something that one has.

*Ich möchte **ein anderes** Bier. Dieses holländische Bier schmeckt mir nicht.* I would like another beer. This Dutch beer doesn't taste good.

13.6 *Kennen, Wissen*

Kennen means "to know, be acquainted with, be familiar with."

Kennst du Berlin? Are you familiar with Berlin?
Kennt ihr seine Romane? Are you familiar with his novels?
Kennt sie seine Freundin? Does she know his girl friend?

Wissen means "to know facts, answers, details."

Weißt du, wo Soest liegt? Do you know where Soest is?
Weißt du, wie viele Romane er geschrieben hat? Do you know
how many novels he has written?
Weiß sie, wie seine Freundin heißt? Does she know his girl
friend's name?

13.7 *Endlich, Schließlich, Zuletzt*

Endlich means "finally" in the sense of "at last."

Er hat uns endlich angerufen. He finally called us.

Schließlich means "finally" in the sense of "at the end of several
stages."

Er hat die anderen zuerst und schließlich mich angerufen. He
called the others first and finally me.

Zuletzt means "finally" in the sense of "last of all."

Zuletzt hat er mich angerufen, ehe er wegging. Finally he called
me, before he went away.

13.8 *Ein paar, Ein Paar*

Ein paar is equivalent to English "several."

Ich habe noch ein paar Fragen. I have a few more questions.

Ein Paar is equivalent to English "a couple" or "a pair."

Sie sind ein glückliches Paar. They are a happy couple.

*Sie hat **ein Paar** Lederhandschuhe.* She has a pair of leather gloves.

13.9 *Treffen, Begegnen, Kennenlernen*

All of these verbs mean "to meet." *Treffen* refers to a planned meeting.

*Ich **treffe** ihn morgen um 7 Uhr.* I am meeting him tomorrow at 7 o'clock.

Begegnen refers to an unplanned meeting.

*Ich **bin** ihr in der Stadt **begegnet**.* I ran into her in town.

Kennenlernen refers to meeting someone in the sense of becoming acquainted.

*Wir **haben uns** in Deutschland **kennengelernt**.* We met/became acquainted in Germany.

13.10 *Es gibt, Es sind*

Es gibt (there is, there are) is followed by the accusative and indicates existence in general and in a large space.

Es gibt weiße Mäuse. There are white mice./White mice exist.

Es sind is more specific and refers to a person or thing clearly defined and in a limited space.

Es sind zwei weiße Mäuse in diesem Zimmer. There are two white mice in this room.

13.11 *Nur, Erst*

Nur means "only" in the sense of "no more than."

*Sie haben **nur** ein Kind.* They have only one child.

Erst implies that more is to come.

*Sie haben **erst** ein Kind.* They have only one child (implying that
they expect more).

13.12   *Lernen, Studieren*

Lernen is equivalent to English "to study" or "to prepare for
class." It also means "to learn a particular skill."

> *Abends müssen die Studenten viel **lernen**.* The students have to
> study a lot in the evenings.

Studieren expresses the act of being a student and of learning
something in depth.

> *Sie **studiert** an Randolph-Macon Woman's College.*
> *Er **studiert** gründlich alle Artikel zu diesem Thema.* He studies
> all articles about this topic thoroughly.

13.13   *Worte, Wörter*

Das Wort has two plurals. The plural for words in context is
Worte.

> *Mit anderen **Worten,** ich verstehe das nicht.* In other words, I
> don't understand that.

The plural for words in isolation is ***Wörter.***

> *Viele Fremd**wörter** stehen in diesem **Wörter**buch.* Many foreign
> words are in this dictionary.

13.14   *Spät, sich verspäten, Verspätung haben*

The adverb ***spät*** (late) can be used with a verb to express the idea
of lateness.

Sie kommt immer zu spät in die Arbeit. She always comes to
   work too late.
Es war zu spät anzufangen. It was too late to begin.

The verb *sich verspäten* (to be late) can be used both for people
and for public transportation.

Der Zug aus Hannover verspätet sich immer. The train from
   Hannover is always late.
Sie wurde entlassen, weil sie sich immer verspätet hat. She was
   fired, because she was always late.

Verspätung haben (to be late) refers only to public transportation.

Der Zug hatte heute zwanzig Minuten Verspätung. The train was
   twenty minutes late today.

13.15 *Ändern, Sich Ändern, Sich Verändern*

The most general of these verbs is *ändern* (to change, alter).

Ich will meine Pläne nicht ändern. I don't want to change my
   plans.
Das läßt sich leider nicht ändern. Unfortunately, that can't be
   changed.

Sich ändern implies an internal change, a change in character or
attitude, a change in the weather, or a change in the times.

Du hast dich geändert. Du bist jetzt viel netter. You have changed.
   You are much nicer now.
*Das Wetter hat sich in den letzten Jahren in dieser Gegend
   geändert.* The weather has changed in the last few years in
   this area.

Sich verändern usually expresses an external change.

75

*Sie **hat sich** sehr verändert. Sie ist viel schöner geworden.* She has changed a lot. She has gotten much more beautiful.

13.16 *Sondern, Aber*

Both *sondern* and *aber* correspond to English "but." *Sondern* is used after a negative statement when the meaning is "rather" or "on the contrary." It contradicts the negative statement.

*Wir waren nicht reich, **sondern** arm.* We were not rich. On the contrary, we were poor.

Aber can also be used after a negative statement, but no contradiction is implied.

*Wir waren nicht reich, **aber** wir waren trotzdem glücklich.* We were not rich, but in spite of that we were happy.

13.17 *Kein* vs. *Nicht*

Kein is the equivalent of *nicht + ein*. It is used to negate nouns preceded by the indefinite article or nothing — but not those preceded by the definite article, which require *nicht*.

*Ich habe **kein** Geld.* I have no money.
*Hast du **einen** Hund? Nein, ich habe **keinen** Hund.* Do you have a dog? No, I do not have a dog.
*Hast du **den** Hund? Nein, ich habe **den** Hund **nicht**.* Do you have the dog? No, I don't have the dog.

Nicht is also used to negate verbs.

*Ich will **nicht** arbeiten.* I don't want to work.

CHAPTER 14

Numerals

14.1 Cardinal Numbers

0	*null*	10	*zehn*	20	*zwanzig*
1	*eins*	11	*elf*	21	*einundzwanzig*
2	*zwei*	12	*zwölf*	22	*zweiundzwanzig*
3	*drei*	13	*dreizehn*	30	*dreißig*
4	*vier*	14	*vierzehn*	40	*vierzig*
5	*fünf*	15	*fünfzehn*	50	*fünfzig*
6	*sechs*	16	*sechzehn*	60	*sechzig*
7	*sieben*	17	*siebzehn*	70	*siebzig*
8	*acht*	18	*achtzehn*	80	*achtzig*
9	*neun*	19	*neunzehn*	90	*neunzig*

100	*(ein) hundert*
1000	*(ein) tausend*
1 000 000	*eine Million*

Note that the numbers from thirteen through nineteen are simply a combination of the numbers three through nine plus ten. The only exceptions are *sechzehn* which drops the *-s* and *siebzehn,* which drops the *-en*. The numbers forty through ninety add *-zig*. Again the *-s* is dropped in *sechzig* and the *-en* is dropped in *siebzig*.

Numbers in German are written as one word, no matter how long.

eintausenddreihundertvierundzwanzig (1,324)

The example above shows that whenever anything follows *eins,* the *-s* is dropped. This also happens when what follows is another word.

Es ist eins. It is one.
BUT
Es ist ein Uhr. It is one o'clock.

14.2 Ordinal Numbers

Ordinal numbers (first, second, third) are formed by adding *-t-* to cardinal numbers under twenty, and *-st-* to twenty and above. Exceptions are *erst-, dritt-, sieb-,* and *acht-* (which adds no extra *-t-*).

1.	*erst-*	7.	*siebt-*
2.	*zweit-*	8.	*acht-*
3.	*dritt-*	9.	*neunt-*
4.	*viert-*	20.	*zwanzigst-*
5.	*fünft-*	21.	*einunzwanzigst-*
6.	*sechst-*	30.	*dreißigst-*

Ordinal numbers are declined like regular adjectives.

Das war unser zweites Gespräch. That was our second conversation.
Das ist das vierte Auto, das vorbeigefahren ist. That is the fourth car that has driven past.
Heute ist der siebzehnte Dezember. Today is the seventeenth of December.

14.3 Days, Months, and Seasons

The gender of the days of the week, the months, and the seasons is masculine.

Days of the Week

der Montag, der Dienstag, der Mittwoch, der Donnerstag, der Freitag, der Samstag/Sonnabend, der Sonntag

Months

der Januar, der Februar, der März, der April, der Mai, der Juni, der Juli, der August, der September, der Oktober, der November, der Dezember

Seasons

der Frühling, der Sommer, der Herbst, der Winter

The German equivalent of English "on" before days of the week is *am*.

Wir treffen uns am Montag. We are meeting on Monday.

Like English, German adds an *-s* to form adverbs with days of the week. As always, adverbs are **not** capitalized.

Wir treffen uns montags. We meet on Mondays.

The German equivalent of English "in" before months and seasons is *im*.

Wir treffen uns im Januar. We are meeting in January.
Wir treffen uns im Winter. We are meeting in the winter.

14.4 Telling Time

For the most part, asking about and telling time in German is similar to English.

Wieviel Uhr ist es?/Wie spät ist as? What time is it? How late is it?
Es ist sieben Uhr. It is seven o'clock.
Es ist sieben Uhr fünfzehn. It is seven fifteen.
Es ist Viertel nach sieben. It is (a) quarter past seven.

Es ist sieben Uhr dreißig.* It is seven thirty.

* It is also common to say:

Es ist halb acht. (literally, It is half of eight.)

Es ist Viertel vor acht. It is (a) quarter to eight.

Es ist Dreiviertel acht. It is (a) quarter to eight (literally, It is three-quarters to eight).

The preposition *um* (at) is used in expressing time of day.

Wir kommen um 5 Uhr. We're coming at 5 o'clock.

In public places, such as train stations and airports, the twenty-four-hour system is used to avoid confusion. It is also used on radio and television. In order to avoid confusing *zwei* and *drei, zwei* is usually pronounced *zwo.*

Der Zug kommt um 18.02 an. The train arrives at 6.02.

14.5 Dates and Age

The question *Welches Datum/Den wievielten haben wir heute?* (What's the date today?) can be answered with either the verb *haben* or the verb *sein.*

Heute haben wir den zwanzigsten Juli or *Heute ist der zwanzigste Juli.* Today is the twentieth of July.

In German, the numerical version of dates follows the pattern of the spoken version, with the date coming before the month — the opposite of the American habit of putting the month first. On a letterhead, the article is in the accusative.

den 31.1. 1993 (1/31 1993)

To give information or to inquire about place and/or date of birth, the past participle *geboren* is used with either the present tense of *sein* or the past tense of *werden*. When referring to the dead, forms of *werden* are always used.

> *Wann **wurde** Bertolt Brecht geboren? Er **wurde** im Jahre 1898 geboren.* When was Bertolt Brecht born? He was born in the year 1898.

When referring to the living, *sein* is used if either the date or place of birth is mentioned.

> *Ich **bin** 1954 geboren.* I was born in 1954.
> *Ich **bin** in Berlin geboren.* I was born in Berlin.

Werden is used when both the date and place of birth are given.

> *Ich **wurde** 1954 in Berlin geboren.* I was born in 1954 in Berlin.

14.6 Time Expressions

Definite time expressions in German are in the accusative unless there is a preposition.

> *Nächsten März fliegen wir nach Deutschland.* Next March we are flying to Germany.

The accusative noun phrase can be replaced by a prepositional phrase in the dative.

> *Im nächsten März fliegen wir nach Deutschland.*

The accusative is also used to express a period of time.

> *Er hat **den ganzen Tag** gearbeitet.* He worked the whole day.

Indefinite time is expressed with the genitive.

Eines Tages ist er einfach verschwunden. One day he just disappeared.

Habitual time is also expressed with the genitive.

Abends habe ich keine Lust zu arbeiten. I don't feel like working evenings.
Wochentags geht er früh schlafen. Weekdays he goes to bed early.

The German equivalents of "tonight," "last night," and "this afternoon" are idiomatic.

Heute abend muß ich arbeiten. Tonight I have to work.
Gestern abend ging ich ins Kino. Last night I went to a movie.
Heute nachmittag erwarte ich Besuch. I am expecting company this afternoon.

Morgen means both "morning" and "tomorrow."

Guten Morgen! Good morning!
Morgen fahren wir nach Hause. Tomorrow we are going home.

"Tomorrow morning" is expressed by *morgen früh.*

Morgen früh besucht er mich. Tomorrow morning he is visiting me.

CHAPTER 15

Basic Vocabulary

15.1 Parts of the Body/Illness

der Kopf (¨-e) –head	*die Brust (¨-e)* –chest
der Mund (¨-er) –mouth	*die Zehe (-n)* –toe
der Bauch (¨-e) –stomach	*die Schulter (-n)* –shoulder
der Finger (-) –finger	*die Hand (¨-e)* –hand
der Rücken (-) –back	*das Gesicht (-er)* –face
der Hals (¨-e) –throat	*das Knie (-)* –knee
der Arm (-e) –arm	*das Auge (-n)* –eye
der Fuß (¨-e) –foot	*das Ohr (-en)* –ear
der Zahn (¨-e) –tooth	*das Haar (-e)* –hair
die Nase (-n) –nose	*das Bein (-e)* –leg

Ich fühle mich nicht wohl. I don't feel well.
Was fehlt Ihnen? What's wrong with you?
Ich habe Kopfschmerzen. I have a headache.
    ...Halsschmerzen – sore throat
    ...Ohrenschmerzen – earache
    ...Magenschmerzen – stomachache
    ...Zahnschmerzen – toothache
    ...Fieber – a fever
    ...Husten – a cough

...Verstopfung – constipation
...Durchfall – diarrhea

Ich möchte bitte etwas gegen Kopfschmerzen usw. I would like
something for a headache, etc.

15.2 Articles of Clothing/Shopping

For women
der BH (Büstenhalter) – bra
die Bluse (-n) – blouse
das Höschen (-) – panties
die Hose (-n) – pants
der Hut (¨-e) – hat
das Kleid (-er) – dress
das Kostüm (-e) – suit
der Mantel (¨-) – coat
der Rock (¨-e) – skirt
der Slip (-s) – slip
die Strickjacke (-n) – cardigan
die (Strümpfe) – stockings
die (Strumpfhosen) – panty hose

For men
der Anzug (¨-e) – suit
das Hemd (-en) – shirt
die Hose (-n) – pants
der Hut (¨-) – hat
die Krawatte (-n) – tie
der Mantel (¨) – coat
der Pullover(-) – sweater
die Socken (-) – socks

Was wünschen Sie bitte? What would you like, please?
Ich möchte einen Pullover. I would like a sweater.
Welche Größe? What size?
Größe 36. Size 36
Welche Farbe? What color?
Wieviel kostet das? How much does that cost?
Gut, ich nehme den/die/das. Good, I'll take that one.

15.3 Colors

beige – beige
blau – blue
braun – brown
mittelbraun – medium brown
gelb – yellow

hell – light
dunkel – dark
hellbraun – light brown
dunkelbraun – dark brown

grau – grey	*hellgrau* – light grey
grün – green	*dunkelgrau* – dark grey
lila – lilac	*hellrot* – light red
orange – orange	*dunkelrot* – dark red
rosa – pink	*rot* – red
bunt – colorful	*schwarz* – black
kariert – checked	*silbern* – silver-colored
gestreift – striped	*violett* – violet
weiß – white	

15.4 Asking and Receiving Directions/ Transportation

Entschuldigen Sie bitte! Excuse me, please.
Wie komme ich zur Bank? How do I get to the bank?
   ...*zur Post* post office?
   ...*zum Bahnhof?* train station?
   ...*zum Hotel Berlin?* Hotel Berlin?
   ...*zum Hof Restaurant?* Hof Restaurant?
   ...*zum Zentrum?* center of town?
   ...*zum Flughafen?* airport?
   ...*zur Bushaltestelle?* bus stop?
   ...*zur Straßenbahnhaltestelle?* street car stop?
   ...*zum Markt?* market place?

Gehen Sie dort links/rechts! Go to the left/right there!
   ...*um die Ecke* – around the corner
   ...*geradeaus* – straight
   ...*in die nächste/erste/zweite Straße links/rechts.* in the next/ first/second street to the left/right.

Fahren Sie mit dem Bus/Taxi/Auto/Zug! Go by bus/taxi/car/train!
   ...*mit der Straßenbahn* – by street car
   ...*mit der U-Bahn* – by subway

15.5 Family

der Vater ("-) – father
das Kind (-er) – child
die Tochter ("-) – daughter
die Schwester (-n) – sister
die Tante (-n) – aunt
die Kusine (-n) – cousin
die Nichte (-n) – niece
der Großvater ("-) – grandfather
die Großmutter ("-) – grandmother
der Schwager ("-) – brother-in-law
die Schwägerin (-nen) – sister-in-law
der Schwiegersohn ("-e) – son-in-law
die Schwiegertochter ("-) – daughter-in-law
die Schwiegervater ("-) – father-in-law
die Schwiegermutter ("-) – mother-in-law

die Mutter ("-) mother
der Sohn ("-e) – son
der Bruder ("-) – brother
der Onkel (-) – uncle
der Cousin (-s) – cousin
der Neffe (-n) – nephew

15.6 Food and Drink/Ordering

Brot – bread
Kuchen – cake

Fisch – fish
Geflügel – poultry
Hühnchen – chicken
Kalbfleisch – veal
Leber – liver
Rindfleisch – beef
Schinken – ham
Schweinefleisch – pork
Speck – bacon

Wurst – sausage
Butter – butter
Joghurt – yogurt
Käse – cheese
Margarine – margarine

Brötchen – roll
Keks – cookie

Blumenkohl – cauliflower
Bohnen – beans
Erbsen – peas
Gurke (-n) – cucumber
Kartoffel (-n) – potato
Kohl – cabbage
Möhre (-n) – carrot
Reis – rice
Rosenkohl – Brussels
    sprouts
Salat – salad; lettuce
Spargel – asparagus
Spinat – spinach
Tomate (-n) – tomato
Zitrone (-n) – lemon

Milch – milk
Sahne – cream

Zwiebel (-n) – onion

Cola
Bier
Wein
Weißwein
Mineralwasser

Rotwein
Kaffee
Tee
Limonade

Apfel (¨-) – apple
Apfelsine (-n) – orange

Birne (-n) – pear
Erdbeere (-n) – strawberry

Kirsche (-n) – cherry
Pampelmuse (-n) –
    grapefruit
Pfirsich (-e) – peach

Herr Ober! Die Speisekarte bitte! Waiter, the menu, please.
Was möchten Sie bitte? What would you like?
Ich hätte gern Hühnchen und Salat bitte. I would like chicken
    and salad, please.
Und zum Trinken? And to drink?
Ein Glas Weißwein bitte. A glass of white wine, please.
Herr Ober! Die Rechnung bitte. Waiter, the check, please.
Getrennt oder zusammen? Separate or together?

15.7 Greetings

Guten Morgen! Good morning!
Guten Tag! Good afternoon!
Guten Abend! Good evening!
Gute Nacht! Good night (when going to bed).
Wie geht es Ihnen? How are you?
Gut, danke, und Ihnen? Fine, thank you. And you?
Auf Wiedersehen! Good-bye.

Glossary

The glossary does not contain the words listed in Chapter 14

aber – but
abfahren – to depart
Adresse, die – address
alle – all
alles – everything
als – than, when
alt – old
an – on
Angestellte, der – employee
Angst, die – fear
anstatt – instead of
antworten – to answer
April, der – April
arbeiten – to work
ärgern, sich...über – to be annoyed about
Arzt, der – doctor
auf – on
August, der – August
aus – out of
außer – besides
Auto, das – car
bei – by, at the home of
begegnen – to meet
Bekannte, der – acquaintance
bestellen – to order
bevor – before
bewegen, sich – to move
Bier, das – beer

Bild, das – picture
bis – until
bleiben – to remain
bringen – to bring
Buch, das – book
da – because
danken – to thank
das – the
daß – that
dein – your
denken – to think
denken an – think of
der – the
deutsch – German (language)
Deutsche, der – German
Dezember, der – December
dich – you
dick – fat
die – the
Dienstag, der – Tuesday
dieser – this
dir – to you
Dom, der – cathedral
Donnerstag, der – Thursday
du – you
durch – through
dürfen – allowed to be
ehe – before
ein, eine – a, an
Einfluß, der – influence
Eltern, die – parents
empfehlen – to recommend
endlich – finally
er – he, it
erzählen – to tell
es – it
essen – to eat

etwas – something
euch – you (acc. and dat.)
euer – your
fahren – to drive
Farbe, die – color
Februar, der – February
Fenster, das – window
finden – to find
fliegen – to fly
Foto, das – photo
fragen – to ask
Fräulein, das – lady (young)
Freitag, der – Friday
Freund, der – friend
freundlich – friendly
Freundschaft, die – friendship
frisch – fresh
für – for
Fuß, zu – by foot
geben – to give
Geburtstag, der – birthday
gefallen – to please
gegen – against
gehen – to go
gehören – to belong to
Geld, das – money
gestern – yesterday
glauben – to believe
glücklich – happy
gratulieren + dat. – to congratulate
groß – big
gut – good
haben – to have
hängen – to hang
Haus, das – house
Hause, zu – at home
heiß – hot

heißen – to be named
helfen – help
Herr, der – gentleman
herrlich – magnificent
heute – today
hinter – behind
hoch – high
Hund, der – dog
ich – I
ihm – to him
ihn – him, it (acc.)
ihnen – to them
Ihnen – to you
ihr – her (possessive), there, to her
Ihr – your
in – in
interessant – interesting
interessieren, sich für – to be interested in
ja – yes
Jahr, das – year
Januar, der – January
jeder – each
Juli, der – July
jung – young
Junge, der – boy
Juni, der – June
kalt – cold
Katze, die – cat
kaufen – to buy
kein, keine, kein – none
kennen – to be acquainted with
Klasse, die – class
kommen – to come
können – can
Konzert, das – concert
kosten – to cost
Krankenhaus, das – hospital

Kuchen, der – cake
Kuh, die – cow
lachen – to laugh
Lampe, die – lamp
Land, das – country
laufen – to run
leben – to live
Leben, das – life
Lehrer, der – teacher
lesen – to read
machen – to do
Mädchen, das – girl
man – one
Mai, der – May
mancher – some
Mann, der – man
Maus, die – mouse
März, der – March
mein – my
meinen – to think
Meinung, die – opinion
Mensch, der – human being
mich – me
mir – to me (dat.)
mit – with
Mittwoch, der – Wednesday
möchten – would like to
Montag, der – Monday
morgen – tomorrow
Morgen, der – morning
Musik, die – music
müssen – must
nach – to (a place), after
Nachbar, der – neighbor
nachher – after
nah – near
Name, der – name

neben – beside, next to
nehmen – to take
nein – no
neu – new
nicht – not
nichts – nothing
Note, die – grade
November, der – November
ob – whether, if
Obst, das – fruit
obwohl – although
oft – often
ohne – without
Oktober, der – October
Paar, ein – pair, couple
paar, ein – several
Professor, der – professor
reich – rich
Reise, die – trip
reparieren – to repair
sagen – say to
Samstag, der – Saturday
schlafen – to sleep
schlank – thin
schließen – to close
schließlich – finally
schnell – fast
schreiben an – to write to
schreiben – to write
Schreibmaschine, die – typewriter
Schule, die – school
Schüler, der – pupil
sehen – to see
sein – to be
sein – his, its
seit – since
September, der – September

setzen, sich – seat (to… oneself)
sie – her, she, it, they, them
Sie – you
singen – to sing
solcher – such
sollen – should (to be supposed to)
sondern – but
Sonnabend, der – Saturday
Sonne, die – sun
Sonntag, der – Sunday
sprechen von – to talk about
sprechen – to speak
statt – instead of
Stock, der – floor
Straße, die – street
Student, der – student
studieren – to study
teuer – expensive
Theater, das – theater
Tisch, der – table
Tourist, der – tourist
tragen – to carry, to wear
treffen – to meet
trinken – to drink
trotz – in spite of
tun – to do
über – above, over
um – around, at
Universität, die – university
uns – us
unser – our
unter – under
Verlobte, der – fiancé
Versicherung, die – insurance
Verwandte, der – relative
viel – much
viele – many

von – from, of
Vorstellung, die – performance
Wagen, der – car
während – during
Wand, die – wall
wann – when
warten auf – to wait for
warum – why
was – what
waschen – to wash
wegen – because of
Weihnachten – Christmas
weil – because
Wein, der – wine
welcher – which
wem – who (dat.)
wen – who (acc.)
wenig – little
wenn – if, when
wer – who (nom.)
werden – to become
wessen – whose
Wetter, das – weather
wie lange – how long
wieso – why
wie viele – how many
wieviel – how much
Wind, der – wind
wir – we
wissen – to know a fact
wo – where
Woche, die – week
wollen – want to
Würde, die – dignity
Wurst, die – sausage
zeigen – to show
zu – to

zuhören – to listen to
zuletot – finally
Zustand, der – condition
zwischen – between

REA's MATH BUILDER

for Admission & Standardized Tests

Specifically designed to prepare you for all tests requiring math ability, including

GRE • GMAT • SAT
GED • ACT • NTE • ELM
PPST • PSAT • CBEST

Research & Education Association

Available at your local bookstore or order directly from us by sending in coupon below.

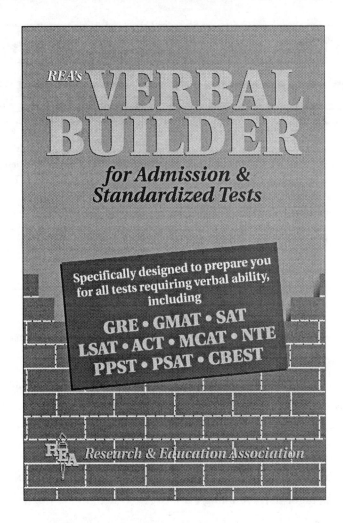

REA's **VERBAL BUILDER**

*for Admission &
Standardized Tests*

Specifically designed to prepare you
for all tests requiring verbal ability,
including

**GRE • GMAT • SAT
LSAT • ACT • MCAT • NTE
PPST • PSAT • CBEST**

REA Research & Education Association

Available at your local bookstore or order directly from us by sending in coupon below.